ME

ME

12-21-06

For Terry —
It's great having you in
Gypsum. Stay - Stay !.

Howard Risk

Howard Risk

To order additional copies of this book, contact:
Xlibris Corporation
1-888-795-4274
www.Xlibris.com
Orders@Xlibris.com
27643

CONTENTS

Dedication

I would like to give credit to Shelly Cash and Claudia Alexander for all of the help they gave me on the computer in the writing of this book . . . and to the gals at the Eagle County Library in Eagle for their help in assisting me through volumes of reference books for information.

PART ONE

CHICAGO

I was raised in a Chicago ghetto by my grandparents. We lived in a run-down dirty, filthy neighborhood infested with rats and mice. Grandpa came from Damascus, Syria—the oldest continuously inhabited city in the world. He would take out his gun and shoot at low-flying birds, or he would buy a lamb's head and bring it home tucked under his arm and put it on the kitchen table for Grandma to cook. It was hairless, its eyes were closed, and its tongue hung out of the corner of its mouth. When I first saw one, I was terrified and ran and hid in the corner. Grandma would come into the room and save me. She would rewrap it and stuff it in the icebox until it was time to eat. As I remember, it was delicious.

I don't remember when it was that I was left with Grandma and Grandpa Ossey. I just remember being there with them and Uncle Jimmie.

If anyone is going to heaven, that someone is Grandma Ossey. I would come home drunk, late at night and pass by her bedroom. I knew she was on her knees praying. I could hear my name mentioned in her prayers. I've locked these memories in my heart.

Grandpa would put on exhibition sword fights at the Palmer House in downtown Chicago. Dressed to the hilt in his fez and vest and donning his famous handlebar mustache, he would cross his arms in front of his chest and introduce himself in Arabic: Saleem from Shem. The audience would be aghast and would ooh and aah. Unsmiling, he and his partner would take up their swords and begin their sham sword fight. Grandpa loved the sound of clashing metal. When it was over, Grandpa would take more than his share of bows and applause. He was a very proud man.

My father died when I was about three years old, and my mother put me in an orphanage. I've blocked out most memories of that place. My mother never came to visit. That's probably when I first began not trusting people. I was left in that horrible place, and there was nothing I could do about it. I was confused. In time, my mother took me to Chicago and left me with my grandparents while she left to remarry. I completely forgot about her.

I have a limited memory of my dad. He would take me by the hand and lead me through neighborhoods where men were tearing up the streets with a jackhammer. I have another memory of my father sitting me on the bed and letting me play with his change and his gold watch. These are the only memories I have of my dad. He died as a result of an operation on his back. From the pictures that I managed to acquire of him, he was an extremely handsome man.

By this time, I had no mother and no father. I was raised on the street. There was no outward affection shown by my grandparents although I didn't doubt Grandma's love. Grandpa cursed in Arabic from the time he got up until the time he went to bed. I can never remember him smiling and having a normal conversation with anyone. In all honesty, he was not a physically violent person.

As time passed, I craved attention and hung out with several gangs. The gang from Farragut High, a motorcycle gang, the gang from Chicago Avenue and for a while, I hung out in several black nightclubs: the Boogie Woogie under the L tracks, the Zanzibar on Ashland Avenue, and the Seventeen Ten Club on Lake Street.

Life was different back then. Rent was twenty dollars a month. A double feature costs a quarter for adults and a dime for children. Restaurants were few and far between, and it wasn't unusual to hear about a mob killing two or three times a month. The mafia fought among themselves for territories, but seldom bothered neighborhood people. There was no television, but most homes had a radio and tuned to Fibber McGee and Molly and Jack Benny. You could get filled up on an order of fish-and-chips at Navy Pier for a quarter. The house you lived in housed your parents and their parents before them, and they all had gone to the same high school. A new house cost several thousand dollars, and a new car a thousand dollars or a little more. Young men hung out on the corner after supper (we call it dinner) and socialized until nine o'clock. Ethnic neighborhoods were made up of Jews, Italians, Poles, Irish, and blacks. Medical insurance was a dollar to fifteen dollars a month, and traveling by streetcar within the city was seven cents for adults and three cents for kids. We had penny candy, and a Baby Ruth costs five cents, haircuts were twenty cents, and a pair of Levi's was three and a half dollars, and everyone knew that the mob controlled the city and accepted it. No one took a shower, we only had bathtubs, and we warmed our house in the winter by stoking the furnace. Phone calls were five cents, and you went through an operator, and your camera of choice was a Kodak box camera. That's the way it was in the forties.

Neighborhood taverns proudly displayed photos of local boys who went to war. Families that made the ultimate sacrifice only had a gold star to hang in their windows.

Bear with me as I try to recall the major events in my life. Actual names in many cases have been intentionally changed, and the sequence of events altered. Omissions are common because many of the people I know are still alive. What I say occurred in 1950 might actually have occurred in 1958 and vice versa, but all events mentioned here are true to the best of my recollection.

Pool halls were where tough guys hung out. There was a pool hall next to the Lindy Theater on Ogden Avenue. Some of the guys would be playing pool, another four or five would be playing poker under a low-hanging light from the ceiling, and Gust, the proprietor, had an eye on everybody to make certain that he collected his five cents from the pool games and drinks. I would look out the front window and see Grandma returning from church, her Bible tucked under her arm, with her inimitable walk. I still have a picture of her in my mind looking down and taking two steps and looking up and repeating the whole thing over. Grandma never suspected that I was hanging out in a pool hall.

I always had a nickel to play the jukebox. This is how I got turned on to jazz and began hanging out at the Boogie Woogie on Twelfth Street. I was accepted by the musicians at the Boogie Woogie, or maybe they just didn't know how to get rid of me, the only white guy in a black club. I would go to their after-hours parties and jam sessions. Sometimes they would send me to the Chicago Theater to bring back sidemen from Woody Herman's Herd or Cab Calloway's Orchestra to jam.

The Boogie Woogie was not in my neighborhood. I had to take the L to get there. I went there often to cover up my loneliness. The club was located under the L tracks on Roosevelt Road, also known as Twelfth Street. When I got to the club, I would go up to the stage and stand all night and listen to the great sounds of Wally Hays and the Moon Rays. The piano player, Willie Jones, and I had a mutual interest in poetry. In between sets, we would sit and discuss the great masters: Shakespeare, Byron, Keats, and the Rubaiyat. As an aside, there was one poem that sticks to my mind. It tells about a sleepy caravan master who entered a village and, upon seeing a grassy area with many caravan masters sleeping, wondered how, upon wakening, he would know himself with so many others asleep. He devised a plan. He took a cord and wrapped it around his toe and thought, *Now I'll know who I am upon awakening.* But another caravan master who overheard his plan untied the cord and put it on his own toe. When our caravan master awakened from his sleep and saw that the cord was around another's toe, he cried out:

Oh good for nothing rascal to perplex me so,
Whether I be I or no.
If I, the cord then why on you,
If you, then where am I, and who.

Around the corner from the Boogie Woogie was the Zanzibar, another black club. I sat at the bar one crowded Saturday night when two plainclothes white cops walked in. All eyes were on them. The music continued. It was obvious they were not welcome. Without saying a word, they began frisking the patrons, starting at one end of the bar and working their way to the end. They got to me and patted me down. At the end of the bar was the men's room. One of them opened the door and reached up over the reservoir and searched with his hand until he took down a gun. That's what they were looking for. They were real pros. They walked slowly to the front door and left. I was into a lot of things by this time.

When someone was playing at the Regal Theater or Savoy Ballroom like "Duke" Ellington or Nat "King" Cole, I would make a special effort to see them. Some of the jitney drivers on South Parkway were not only driving their vehicles to pick up and deliver their passengers, but were also selling drugs. They would drive back and forth on South Parkway and pick up and deliver passengers for a fee of five cents a pop.

Mummy and Nick the Greek used to hang out with Uncle Jim on Kedzie and Sixteenth. They were both drafted but never came back from the war alive. I gave them the best five-cent shoeshine I could muster up when they came to the house on Saturday evenings to wait for Uncle Jim to get ready.

No town in America was more generous to our GIs than Chicago during World War II. If a GI went into a restaurant, the meal was on the house. If they tried to pay their way on a streetcar, it was on the house. If they wanted to see a play, it was on the house. Everything was on the house to our men in uniform during World War II.

I love Chicago. I hate Chicago. I have good memories. I have bad memories. The bad memories are of the filth and dirt and corruption. The good memories are of family and friends. Living in Chicago, I learned to doubt and not to trust, to be leery and skeptical, to be alert and to keep my back to the wall, and to keep a two-dollar bill in my wallet for the cops in case I get stopped. Show your driver's license to some Chicago cops, and if he sees the tip of the two-dollar bill he'd slip it out of your wallet and you'd be on your way. That's the way it was in the '40s. I learned to say "I don't know nuttin' about nuttin'" when questioned by the police. That was one way of staying out of trouble.

The JPI on Douglas Boulevard was the center for Jewish activities in the neighborhood. I'm not certain what *JPI* stood for, so we assumed it meant Jewish

People's Institute. Most of the community was made up of Jews. When there was a Jewish holiday, the teachers would tell the gentile kids that if our parents wanted to take us out of school for any reason, that would be a good time to do it because it would be futile for them to attempt to teach four or five gentile kids and leave forty Jewish kids behind.

A Jewish bookie on Roosevelt Road bragged that he didn't have an enemy in the world. That very night, he was gunned down.

One of my Jewish friends invited me to his house after school. I turned around when I heard footsteps and saw an elderly lady with a cane. Julius edged closer to me and whispered, "Tell her you're Jewish."

We all got out of school at the same time, but then the Jewish kids would go to shul where they were taught Hebrew and learned Jewish culture. The Jews were quite clannish and hung out together. The gentile kids never had a problem with the Jewish kids. We all got along fine.

Hungry men would walk up the back stairs and beg Grandma for a slice of bread or anything else she could spare. Grandma always had something for these poor unfortunates. The men were always grateful for the least handout.

The Huddle was a restaurant on Kedzie and Ogden that had a sign in the window that read, "If you are hungry and have no money, come in. We will feed you free." Times were tough. Al Capone had set up soup kitchens all over Chicago. Don't ever say anything bad about Big Al. He had a good reputation. You couldn't ask for a better neighbor than a member of the mafia. They could get things done for you in a heartbeat that might take you or me months or years. But don't cross them. They make bitter enemies. Everyone knew that the mob controlled the city.

Western Electric in Cicero had thirty-nine thousand employees. Many of them played the horses at the many bookie joints right across the street from Western Electric. There were two racetracks in Cicero. On our break and on our lunch hour, we would go to the window and watch as the Cicero police went from a barbershop to a tavern to a flower shop to get paid off. They were all bookies. Occasionally, there would be a complaint from a Joe Citizen who heard about the bookies and wanted to put them out of business. The police would stage a phony raid, pay the bookies a couple bucks, keep them for a couple of hours, and release them. The newspapers would do a piece on how the Cicero police broke up a crime ring right across the street from Western Electric. Now the citizens were happy, the bookies were happy, and the police were happy, and the bookies were back in business with police approval.

There was a shooting a block from our house on south Sawyer. A policeman was shot and killed by a mobster on the L platform. Blood dripped down between the boards of the L platform. Neighbors came running. Pretty soon there was a crowd, and everyone was asking, "What happened?" There were conflicting reports until morning.

There was a guy I worked with at Western Electric that I'll call the Scrounger. He could get anything you wanted or needed for a price. Just tell him what you needed, and in due time, he would notify you that he had your item—tools, auto engine or parts, typewriters, a pet, or whatever. Of course, everything was hot.

Uncle Jim took me with him to vote. As he shook hands with the registrar, the registrar slipped him a couple of dollars to vote a certain way. I grew up thinking that you accepted money to vote.

Uncle Ed hired a horse and buggy to haul coal to our house. He put the coal into heavy-duty canvas bags and then hoisted it on his back and dumped it in the buggy. Then he drove the buggy to our house, unloaded it at the basement window, and shoveled it into the basement where we used it in the furnace.

Vendors went through the alleys with horse-drawn buggies selling their wares or wanting to buy your old iron and rags. "Rags 'n' iron," they would call out. "Buy your old rags 'n' iron." Or if they were selling strawberries, they'd call out, "Strawberries. Get your fresh strawberries." Of course they had other fruits and vegetables to sell you once they lured you down to see their strawberries.

Huge horse-drawn troughs were towed through the alleys to collect the garbage. Men with shovels would scoop up the garbage and toss it into the trough and later dump the garbage in a common landfill.

Grandpa would give me two cents and an empty pitcher to go to the local deli to have the pitcher filled with flavored carbonated water. If I had a penny or two left over, I'd buy a picture of Mickey Rooney or Judy Garland.

There were three police cars that I remember distinctly from the old neighborhood: 127, 48, and 148. I don't remember anyone ever calling them. We usually took matters into our own hands to do whatever had to be done to resolve a nasty situation. One evening, I was picked up by 127 and taken to the police station for questioning. I was accused of smuggling guns into the neighborhood and raping nurses. One detective took out a rubber hose and paced back and forth in front of me, slapping his hand with the hose and uttering, "We got ways of making guys like you to talk." I wasn't scared, just annoyed by this overgrown idiot accusing me of smuggling and raping. They had picked up another guy who had done nothing either and accused him of crimes he had not committed. He went around dressed in a cowboy outfit: holster, chaps, gun and all the rest of Western attire. He called himself Gene Autry. The police were having a good old time with him, challenging him to a mock gunfight when one of them took out Gene Autry's gun. His jaw dropped when he realized that the gun was real. Everyone stopped clowning around. They took him into a room for interrogation and completely forgot about me.

I've blocked out all memories of the holidays while growing up in Chicago.

I worked at Union Station in downtown Chicago with six or seven friends. We were breaking into luggage and stealing anything we could get our hands on: cameras, cigarettes, jewelry, and perfumes. We could get into most pieces of luggage in five seconds. Because the items we stole were to be transported across state lines, it was a federal offense, and the Federal Bureau of Investigation (FBI) stepped in.

I was in bed on a Saturday morning when Grandma came into my room and woke me up. She said that there were two schoolteachers here to see me. It was the FBI. They walked into the bedroom and identified themselves. While I was getting dressed, one of them asked me about a gun that, he heard, was in my possession. I went to the clothes closet and reached into a packet of clothes and produced the gun. I handed it to the agent. They told me that I had to go with them and make a statement. Grandma was confused about the gun and the FBI badges. She didn't know what to believe. Poor Grandma.

They took me downtown to the federal building where I made my statement and was photographed. One of the agents stood by during the questioning. Their questions were simple and easy, and my answers were simple and easy. I thought of the robberies as more of an act of mischief than anything else, but I had violated federal laws.

I was put in a cell that was in the middle of the room. There were no walls, just bars on all four sides. I heard my name called out by another prisoner. It was someone from the Boogie Woogie. We greeted each other, and later I was released, and the two FBI agents drove me home. I was treated royally by the FBI. There was never a time when I thought I could have been treated better.

A cigar-smoking, fat lawyer read about our arrest in the paper and came knocking on our door to represent me at the trial. My family realized the enormity of the case and got a couple hundred dollars together and paid the lawyer who did absolutely nothing for me. We were each given three-year probations and had to report to a federal probation officer once a month.

For some strange reason, I went back to Union Station and a girl employee who had obviously read the papers saw me and got panicky. She called out to the Military Police, "That's him. That's him. Put him in jail, the guy in the paper." She overreacted. When she got the attention of an MP, he tried to calm her down and explain that everything had been taken care of. She kept yelling, and the MP just walked away.

The local Chicago police read about us in the paper and picked me up and put me in jail. Someone called the FBI, and they came and got me out of jail and apologized for the dumb action of the Chicago police. This happened before we went to trial. The Chicago police were overstepping their boundaries.

While I was still working at Union Station, part of our job was handling canvas mailbags. When we got a break, we would make comfortable beds out of them and lay across several of them to rest. I looked up and saw two huge men in heavy winter coats and hats handcuffed to each other. I could tell who the bad guy was. The prisoner looked down at me and asked, "Hey, kid, ya gotta cigarette?" The cop nudged him to be quiet. They were on the way to the penitentiary to leave the bad guy off.

For thirty-five cents, you could get an order of short ribs and fries at Sally's Bar BQ on Drake and Ogden. For another dime, you could get an order of long ribs. I never knew the difference. Without missing a beat or looking up, Harry, the fountain man, would pitch you. "You need a pair of shoes, a ring, a set of encyclopedias, a radio? Go downstairs. Someone will take care of you." Of course, everything was hot.

Up the street from Sally's, on the corner was McGuire's. There were always police cars at the curb while the cops were inside playing cards.

I went home with another friend from school who took me down to his basement to show me something. He opened the furnace door and reached in and took out a string-wrapped package. He unwrapped it and took out a tommy gun. We both hefted it, and for a brief moment, we were big shots. He rewrapped it and put the bundle back. His father was in the mob.

Old men, usually of foreign ancestry, were hired by the city to keep the streets clean. They were given shovels and brooms and a route to work. What a great way to utilize the senior population and to give them a sense of worth.

I wasn't a big shot by any means, but I did have street savvy. I knew the right people, and they knew me. A stranger would stand out like a sore thumb.

The Lawndale Bible Church had a great spiritual impact on my life. All of this time, I had a strong belief in God, but I still did my thing. When things got rough, I prayed to God and acknowledged his presence. As time went on, I studied the Bible more. All because of Grandma.

There was a garage next door to the Lindy Theater on Ogden Avenue. I would see a black mechanic take cars out of the garage and drive them to the curb and work on them. One day, two cars sped into the garage, the doors closed; then the three police cars from the neighborhood pulled up to the curb, and the officers went into the garage. About two hours later, the police walked out of the garage to their respective cars and drove away. I deduced that there were some negotiations, and the cops and the other guys came to terms. But I didn't see nuttin' and didn't know nuttin'.

You can walk by someone at night and be challenged. "Hey, you. What's your name?" If it's Italian, and Italians are out of favor that week, chances are you'll get beaten up. Or if you're Jewish or Irish or Polish or whatever. It's best to say your name is Jones or Smith.

Lower Wacker Drive is in the downtown area. You're actually below the street level. The cops challenged a sixteen-year-old driver. He pulled out a gun and started shooting at the officers. The officers shot back and killed him. The boy's father used to chain him to the bed and beat him. His teachers said that he was a quiet, obedient boy.

When you went into a restaurant in Chicago, chances are the tablecloths, the silverwares, cups, and saucers were all supplied by the mob. If the owner chose not to use mob accessories, he would get his legs broken.

Grand Avenue and Taylor Street were a mecca for people of Italian descent. We would drive to Grand Avenue and seek out a little Italian man pushing a cart down the street who would sell you the most delicious Italian sausage sandwich with broiled green peppers dipped in sausage grease for twenty-five cents. Appropriately enough, there was a funeral parlor on the corner where mafia members would be laid to rest.

The hamburger joint on Damen and Chicago Avenues was a late, after-hours hangout. Three guys came running in past the waitress and headed toward the kitchen. None of the patrons said or did a thing. Two uniformed policemen ran in right after them. They asked if anyone saw three men run into the restaurant. Nobody knew nuttin' about nuttin'. With guns drawn, they walked into the kitchen. About two minutes later, they left through the front door empty-handed.

Every six months, you had to apply for a safety sticker for your car. They would test your brakes, horn, lights, and any other safety feature. I flunked the first three times I went through until someone wised me up. "You gotta pay the inspector off." But of course. The next time I went through the line, I left a two-dollar bill hanging out of my wallet. When it was time to show the inspector my driver's license, he slipped the two dollars out of my wallet and punched my card. I had passed.

Uncle Jim was explaining the art of stamp collecting when his brother, Eddie, walked into the room. I could see that Eddie had been crying. He bent over Uncle Jim and said, "Jimmie, why won't you talk to me? What did I do?" Without looking up, Uncle Jim said, "Get out of my sight." Uncle Eddie started to cry and left the room. I realized that there was bad blood between them. Those were the only words I ever heard them speak to each other. I got along well with Uncle Eddie and his family. On the other hand, I got along well with Uncle Jimmie. There must have been some brotherly love between them because one night, there was a disturbance outside our bedroom window. I heard the name Eddie mentioned. Uncle Jim jumped out of bed and went to his toolbox and took out a pair of brass knuckles. He dressed and ran outside. About half an hour later, he returned, put the brass knuckles back in the toolbox, and, without saying a word, went to bed.

I got curious one day and searched Uncle Jim's effects without him knowing it. I reached up on his closet shelf and felt a sock. It felt firm as if something was in it. I unwrapped it and discovered a snub-nosed revolver. I felt it and hefted it and wrapped it and put it back. My curiosity was satisfied.

At about age five, I became ill and was confined to my bed. I remember having a high fever. In a delusional state, I was being chased by elephants and tigers and lions. I yelled out in my sickness and screamed for the animals not to catch me. Many years later in a psychology class, I read that children who had severe emotional problems due to lack of a stable home life often became ill and experienced the same type of delusions.

The cops loved to raid a dice game on a corner or in an alley. I lived two flights up on South St. Louis. Dice games were often held in the alley right below our apartment. I became an unauthorized spotter and would warn the players when I saw the cops coming. When the police drove by and saw the players, they would make a lot of noise to scare them away. They weren't interested in catching any of the players, but in picking up and keeping the money.

Chicago used to be quite prejudiced. A lot of hotheads were running around in Cicero and Berwyn where most of the residents were Polish or Czech. They tried to keep people of color out. Of course, there were riots. There was a front-page picture in *Life Magazine* of a gang of bare-chested men marching defiantly toward the camera. I knew one of the men in the frontline of the mob.

Gang members from the north side were out to stick up somebody. They waited until their patsy came, surrounded him, and warned him not to scream. They took him to an alley and relieved him of his coat and money and had him count to a hundred. They laughed when they told me about it. None of them had real guns at the time, but it wasn't long before they were carrying real guns and sticking up liquor stores and gas stations.

There was a dimly lit club on Ogden Avenue where the job of the girls were to get visiting men drunk and lead them to a booth, where their male accomplices would relieve the men of their wallets. The way I had it figured, a good-looking young girl fresh from the farm, looking for excitement, met a man who wooed her and promised her a good time. He got her hooked on drugs and became her pimp. He also became her source of drugs. She would do anything for him: sell herself, steal for him, and buy drugs from him.

One of the older guys in the neighborhood would buy a carload of carnations and drive me around the suburbs and skid row and any place where there was nightlife. I would go into a club and sell a gardenia for a quarter a pop. After a while, I figured he was making a killing. He paid me a total of five or six bucks for the entire night, and he kept all of the tips. It wasn't long before I wised up and began putting the tips in my shoe and giving him a small portion of them. Now when I went home and counted all of my money, I had close to forty dollars.

Crazy and I went into a bar and noticed two cops playing pool in the back behind sheer curtains. They were plainclothes cops with their guns strapped around their chests. They stopped playing and eyed us. We eyed them. Everyone froze. They were thinking, "These guys don't look kosher." After a beat or two, we left.

Grandma went to work for Nabisco on Randolph Street. Nabisco went on strike, but Grandma crossed the picket line and was given twenty dollars by her bosses. She put food on our table.

During the army draft, I volunteered to join the army and saw some very interesting things. A young man had been turned down for physical reasons. He laughingly waved his rejection papers in the face of one of the girls working at the draft board. She was not happy with him and grabbed the papers from him and stamped "Accepted" on them. I don't know how she got away with that.

A torpedo (gunman) came to the side door of a tavern close to where I hung out on Chicago Avenue and shot a guy sitting at the bar. It was a mob killing. The bartender knew it was coming and walked away from the victim when the torpedo walked in. After a beat or two, the bartender did his duty and called the cops. Even if you knew the shooter, you would never say anything to the cops. Shooters are never after you or me.

I couldn't make out any of the guys in the car that had just pulled up to the corner, but evidently, Lefty knew them. He walked over and greeted them. Later, he told me that they asked about me. They wanted to know if I was okay. Lefty assured them that I was. They told Lefty that they were looking for the guy who was going out with their brother's girlfriend. They had a hammer and were going to beat the guy with it.

The *mish* was short for mission. It was open only on Saturday nights to the neighborhood. We listened to sermons and sang hymns; then everyone went downstairs where we had refreshments and worked on our hobbies.

Crazy became more brazen and daring. He killed a girl, but there was a witness who went to the police. Meanwhile, he joined the military and went before the judge in uniform. The judge dismissed the case. The word on the street was that Crazy had paid the judge a couple of hundred dollars to dismiss the case. Crazy had a vicious, violent temper. I've seen him threatening the life of a proprietor of a business if he didn't get the service he thought he was entitled to.

Maxwell Street is the place to shop on Sunday afternoons when the merchants put their wares out on the street for you to examine. It was the precursor of today's flea market. I picture one merchant putting his wares out on the sidewalk to be closer to the buyer. His fellow merchants did the same, and pretty soon, everyone was in the middle of the street. There's nothing you can't buy on Maxwell Street. If you park a block or two from Maxwell Street and someone offers to sell you a set of tires for your car that are just the right size, beware. They could already be from your car. Female gypsies inhabit the storefronts on Maxwell Street and will knock loudly on the windows to get your attention. They'll promise you a good time for fifty cents. But when you go inside, they'll rob you.

When Joe Louis became the heavyweight champion of the world, he came to Chicago. All of the blacks on Lake Street turned out for their hero. Armed men stood on rooftops to protect their man. They were leery of all white men who came within an uncomfortable distance of their champ.

You could reach out of your window and touch the L if you lived that close to its route. It had a high-pitched, rusty squeal as it made its turns, especially as it entered and exited the loop.

Uncle Jim hurried into the basement and fiddled with the furnace. I knew something was wrong because of his quick and sudden movements. He threw open the furnace door after examining the gauges. Evidently, the gauges read too high, and the furnace could have exploded had he not gotten there when he did.

I looked out the front window at six o'clock in the morning on a ten-below-zero day and saw my mother waiting to catch the bus to take her to work at Zenith Radio. Mom did her best. She saw to it that we had food on the table and a roof over our heads. It's too bad that appreciation often comes too late.

At night, we could hear the rats in the walls scratching to get out. Dead rats have a distinct odor. When we played games at night and ran through the alleys, we would kick squealing rats as we ran. When we went to the Lindy Theater, we would have to keep our feet up on the seats in front of us. Otherwise, the rats would rub up against our legs, searching for popcorn.

State and Madison streets were known as the "Crossroads of the World." On an exceptionally frigid day I heard my name called. "Hey, Blackie," it was Mojo, a guy from the neighborhood. He danced over to me in his heavy-duty winter coat and explained that he was looking for crapshooters. He had a few players in a hotel room but he needed a few more. He was stopping men on the street to see who might be interested. A few more would do it. I didn't stick around long enough to see if he had any luck.

Uncle Wolf brought me a box of clothes at Christmas while I was in the orphanage. I wouldn't have to cover the holes in my shoes with cardboard, and I finally had a hat with flanges to keep my ears warm on severely cold days. Uncle Wolf was the only person that came to visit me on Sundays at the orphanage after he put in twenty hours a day in his store. He sat next to me in the lounge until he began nodding and would fall sound asleep.

Grandma came to my bedroom door one morning and asked, "Guess who's here?" My mother stepped out from behind the door. All of a sudden, I became very confused. Should I run to her? Should I kiss her? I did neither. I said nothing. She was back to stay. I continued living with my grandparents while my mother got housing in the area. I never did ask her where she had been or why she was back or for how long. I thought about it, but I was afraid to ask.

An innocent guy is sometimes fingered to do time in jail for a mobster. If he's smart, he'll do the time. Otherwise, he's dead. His wife will get a check every month from the mob, and when he gets out, he's got a job for life with the mob.

We lived three flights up on South Central Park. Our insurance agent would come around faithfully every month, cigar in his mouth, and would huff and puff climbing three flights of stairs to collect his fifty-cent insurance premiums.

I think of Chicago as having always been there: the same streets, the same alleys, the same ghettos, the same Navy Pier, and the same mob.

I guess we were poor. I had no concept of poor. Some had and some didn't. Men would say, "God bless you Al" to Al Capone. When they stood in one of Big Al's soup lines, they didn't care what the papers said about Al. Their stomachs were being filled.

We didn't have the lousy two dollars to pay the electric bill, so they turned off our electricity. Uncle Jim removed the solder from the unit and restored power until he heard that the power company was coming. Then he would put everything back the way it was supposed to be.

Uncle Jim assembled birdcages for a living. On Saturdays, I would go down to where he worked and get a dime from him to go to the movies. I would be able to see two full-length movies, three cartoons, a serial, and an amateur show on stage, get a free ice cream bar, and a pass to come back the following Thursday. A dime went a long way.

Another way of getting movie money was to go junking. I would go up and down alleys and examine garbage to find brass, copper, or iron. I would take what I find to Mike, the junkman, who weighed it and gave me what it was worth, about fifteen or twenty cents. The screw-in part of a discarded light bulb was good, as well as the insulated wire once the insulation had been burned off. I got more for copper, less for brass, and much less for iron.

I had no trouble surviving physically, but emotionally, I did. Sometimes, I imagined I was someone else and doing quite well when in fact I was hurting inside. There was no one I could talk to or confide in. I made some dumb, stupid decisions. I could have turned to the family, but they wouldn't have understood. There were a number of escapes that I used. I went to downtown Chicago where I sat in the radio audience of *That Brewster Boy*, or I would go to see a Blackhawk hockey game or the roller derby or to the Field Museum, Goldblatts, or Grant Park. Always alone.

When Crazy was nineteen, he was arrested for hijacking. He made a futile attempt at escaping from the Twenty-Sixth Street Jail. I finally realized that I wanted nothing more to do with him.

Wrigley Field was my favorite major league ballpark as a kid. Avid baseball fans lived in the tenement houses that surrounded the park and could see all of the games free from their windows with a beer in hand.

As I walked down Sixteenth Street, I would pass Hebrew butchers who had de-feathered chickens hanging by their necks from hooks and a stack of newspapers in which to wrap the chickens. If you want a delicious portion of meat, buy it from a Hebrew butcher. They're known for their excellent choices.

The bakery near our house refused to join the union. One night, there was a terrific explosion. The next morning, we walked over to Kedzie Avenue to see what had happened. A pile of rubble stood where the bakery had been. The machinery inside was a mass of twisted metal lying all over the floor and imbedded in the walls. The owner soon joined the union.

Lake Street was the dividing line between where the blacks could live and where they couldn't live. If a black went north of Lake Street, his life would be in jeopardy. I never understood this.

The Black brothers were fresh from the farm and had a reputation for being real tough guys. I had a nodding acquaintance with them. Everyone knew that after dark, they would go out and strong-arm people for their money. At first, I was afraid of them, but a few things happened to make me think that they were just as much afraid of me as I was of them. We left one another alone.

God had his hand over me in Chicago. I hung out in some pretty tough neighborhoods, but I was never threatened or attacked or had to fight. I prayed a lot and not just when I was in trouble. The best thing that Grandma ever did was to take me to a Bible-teaching church where the Word of God was preached. I got away from the church for a while, but at least now I had a firm foundation in the Word, and I knew right from wrong.

I found a note from one of Grandpa's paramours. It stated, "We better stop seeing each other. Your wife is bound to find out."

None of Grandpa's children ever showed love toward one another. I believe that Uncle Eddie showed more love than any of the others. It was not an outwardly loving family. I did see displays of love from Grandpa toward some of his distant relatives, but not for his wife and children.

Art was a jazz buff and a good friend. He wore Coke bottle glasses. We would go to his house, and he would put on records and play the drums. When he didn't show up for a while, I became concerned and contacted him. He had crushed his little finger on machinery at work while he was high. We resumed our friendship and began getting together and playing records and talking jazz.

Wherever Grandma was, she was contented. I visited her once in their store on Homan Avenue. She had pinned up a sheet over the door separating the front of the store from the back and was quite content as long as she had her Bible. Grandma learned well the biblical saying, "Learn to be content in whatever circumstances you find yourself."

We moved around quite a bit in those days. My grandparents thought I was at my mother's, and my mother thought I was at my aunt's. Meanwhile, the gang from Farragut decided to run away and join the merchant marines. We got picked up on the highway by a sheriff and put in jail while he did some checking on us. I met another prisoner while in jail with whom I had a lot in common with. We both loved the blues, and we sang our hearts out:

"Going to Chicago, I got the blues; and I'm as blue as I can be."

In time, parents came to get their kids. When I got home, I figured surely someone would have missed me. I'd have given anything if someone would have said, "Where have you been?" No one said a word.

There was a large family of gypsies that were stuck in the neighborhood during the war. Some of the men hung out at the local pool hall. I bonded with several of the men and went out nightclubbing with them. In one place that we went to, the bartender tried to hustle us. Every five minutes, he came to our table and asked, "Watcha havin', Mac?" I hadn't finished my first drink yet.

Pat and I both got jobs working in a whiskey warehouse. We would board our respective trucks early in the morning, and for the rest of the day, our drivers would drive to taverns all over town. Our job was to deliver the liquor inside the clubs. I usually went with the driver who had skid row on his route. It wasn't unusual to drop a box and break a few bottles while getting it off the truck. If we were on skid row and that happened, a bum would come running and lie on his back under the box and drink from the leaking box as we lifted it back into the truck.

When we entered a club in the morning, there was always a strong odor of urine and beer. The chairs would be upside down on the table to allow the janitor to sweep around it. The owner would be at the cash register counting the night's receipts.

Grandpa would write on a brown paper bag the amount of money owed him from a transaction and the name of the purchaser and pin it up on a nail on the wall.

The north side gang wore zoot suits. I bought one and wore it. We stood on the corner of Leavitt and Chicago in a group and looked for trouble. We would go to Grand Avenue and let it be known that we were looking for a fight by going into their territory. I would never want to go on these forays and made excuses not to go. Occasionally, when we went into another territory, some of the guys I was with knew some of the residents in that neighborhood, and we wound up socializing and not fighting. This was before anyone was married, and we were free spirits.

On Saturday, the Jewish Sabbath, I would work on my motorcycle. A Hassidic Jew came by one Saturday and waved his long bony finger at me and reprimanded me for working on the Sabbath, thinking I was Jewish. I got on my motorcycle and drove away.

The racetrack held a fascination for me. I was winning quite a bit of money, but the stress was too much, and I decided to give it up. I would go to Del Mar

Race Track on the train, spend the day there and not get home until nine o'clock at night. Then I would sit on my bed and sort out my winnings and go right back the next day. That was the positive side. The negative side was losing over and over. It became too stressful, and I decided to give it up.

I have vague, hazy memories of many of the incidents that occurred during my growing-up years in Chicago, and other things I remember as if they happened yesterday. For example, I can't remember the holidays while growing up at all. I recall incidents but can't recall when they happened, yesterday or twenty years ago.

The gang from Farragut High hung out at Krejcis on Twenty-sixth Street. It was the center of activity for the after school kids. One evening, two guys from school came in and left shortly afterward. The next day, in the paper, the main news item was about a stickup at a club in Lyons by two young men. It wasn't just any club. It was a mob hangout. And it wasn't just a mob hangout, but it was mob bookie joint. Everyone knows that at the end of the day, bookies have a lot of cash on hand. The stickup guys knew when to hit it. A couple of days later, the police found the bodies of the stickup men in a quarry. It was the same two men who came into Krejcis a couple of nights before.

I was hurting a lot of girls, and this hurt me, so I backed off when I realized that I could not handle affairs of the heart. For the longest time, females were just toys. I was very confused but preoccupied with girls.

After my father died and my mother left me, any girl or woman that I came to know or like scared me to death. I was afraid that she was going to leave me just as my mother did. After extended therapy and being given tools to work with, I became quite comfortable around women. I became a flirt, but way down deep inside, I still had fear of rejection.

Years later, when Grandpa passed away, I was living in Los Angeles and flew back to Chicago for the funeral. All of the cousins met at the funeral parlor on Sacramento Boulevard. On the second floor of the funeral parlor, a gangster was laid out after meeting an untimely gangland death. Cousin Leonard knew some of the deceased's relatives that came to pay their respects to the deceased. His widow brought in bottles of liquor. She was a gorgeous lady dressed in stark black.

Grandma cried at Grandpa's funeral. She sat all alone in Aunt Mabel's basement. No one comforted her, not even me.

When we lived on South St. Louis, we had an Italian landlord who made Dago Red in our basement. Dago Red is homemade red wine that is super delicious and you should feel honored when your Italian friends give you a bottle. Our landlord came to our house with some Italian men and went down to the basement in the early afternoon. The longer they stayed, the noisier they became. By midnight, they were dancing and singing songs in Italian. They were drinking their homemade brew and were thoroughly inebriated. They left sometime after midnight, but they did give Grandpa a few bottles of Dago Red.

Taylor and Halsted Streets were very dangerous areas, but it was where one could buy any ethnic food or ingredient that one wanted. Grandma used to go down to Taylor and Halsted and buy her Syrian foods: *snobar*, tahini, grape leaves, and bulgur. There were stores that supplied foods for the Turks, Germans, Poles, Greeks, and many more. That was when bulgur came in five grades, and it was delivered in barrels.

On the south side of town, around Thirty-first and South Park, which was black territory, was a poolroom. On hot summer nights, men would gather outside just to have a place to socialize and drink beer. One of the men was a cop who would sell you any amount of dope you wanted.

Freeze and I would hop on the L and go to the south side, Forty-seventh and South Park to be exact. Forty-seventh and South Park was strictly black, and it was where the Regal Theater and the Savoy Ballroom were located. We would get off the L and walk down side streets until we got to our destination, usually a rundown residence or apartment building. We gave a secret knock, were identified, and then the door would open slowly, and we were let in. In the corner were steps, and at the top of the steps was a statue of the Virgin Mary, which was their omen for good luck. They took us downstairs where three musicians were playing. Introductions were in order, and then Freeze would sit down at the drums. He played on and off for about four hours, and he was very good. He mouthed most of the music all the way back home and walked with a dippy rhythm, black style. Our musical needs were satisfied until the next time.

I was now eighteen years old.

PART TWO

MOTORCYCLES

I knew some of the bike riders that hung out at Krejcis, so when it got right down to it, I had to have one. I collected my savings and bought a military bike in a crate and put it together. In no time, I was hanging out with all of the bikers in the suburban bike hangouts. There was Tiger, Big Wally, Deadhorse, Bambi, Little Mike, Big John, Blackie, Tut, Red, and Duck. We hung out at Shorty's in Lemont, Wally and Gene's in Cicero, and all of the bike hangouts in between. We were avid beer drinkers.

Shorty's place was my favorite hangout. It was far enough out in the country so that a serious beer drinker could raise a little hell and not be hassled by the police. Shorty's had no neighbors. The place was right across the highway from a cemetery, and Shorty often said, when his neighbors complained about the noise, that he was moving. When his customers had to go to the bathroom, Shorty would point to twenty acres out back and tell them to pick a tree. His son Guydy would drink all of the leftover beer and wine that the customers left on the bar. He was all of seven years old.

Wally and Gene's was a favorite bike hangout in Cicero, right off of Ogden Avenue. The jukebox played country-and-western music, and we danced and stomped our boots on the wooden floor and sang along with the jukebox,

"Cigareettes, rye whuskey and wild, wild women-they'll drive you crazy, they'll drive you insane."

One late night at Wally and Gene's, someone was playing dice with Wally to see who would buy the next round of drinks. Wally called the dice differently than his opponent. An argument started. The music was very loud. Someone saw Wally go behind the bar and get a gun and yelled for him to go outside and cool down.

Me and Shorty

POLICE CHARGE WOMAN WITH MURDER ATTEMPT

Two Taverns Closed As Result of Shooting Scrape

A 23-year-old man was shot in the right leg by a woman early Friday morning in front of the Bridge Side Inn, 5125 W. 29th st.

The man, Edmund Jarecki, 2824 Cermak rd., was shot by Barbara Wakefield, who owns a tavern at 5036 W. 29th pl. Jarecki was taken to Hines Hospital where his condition is reported as good.

According to Lt. Lester Connerty, head of the detective bureau, the shooting took place when Jarecki approached Wally Charvat, owner of the Bridge Side Inn, to ask him to replace the pistol he had taken from the back of the bar.

At this point Barbara Wakefield appeared on the scene and told Jarecki to mind his own business and took the gun from Charvat. Jarecki told Lt. Connerty that she fired without warning.

After she fired the shot a tavern patron, Howard Risk, 1553 S. Central Park ave., Chicago, rushed outside and tried to take the gun away from her. In the struggle the gun went off again, but the bullet went wild.

Patrons in the tavern had told Jarecki that Charvat had taken the gun from the back bar and placed it in his pocket.

The Bridge Side Inn and the Wakefield tavern have been closed by the police.

Two charges have been filed against Barbara Wakefield, assault and attempt to commit murder with a deadly weapon. She is out on a $5,000 bond. The charges were preferred by Risk and Jarecki.

BIND PUB OWNER TO GRAND JURY

Woman Accused of Shooting Chicagoan

Barbara Wakefield, Cicero tavern owner who was arrested on September 2 in the shooting of a 23-year-old Chicagoan, was bound over to the grand jury in Cicero police court Thursday on a charge of assault with a deadly weapon.

Walter Charvat, owner of the Bridge Side Inn, 5125 W. 29th st., where the shooting took place, was fined $200 and costs when he admitted there had been gambling in the pub prior to the assault.

Edmund Jarecki, 2824 Cermak rd., was shot by Barbara Wakefield in front of the tavern after he asked Charvat to replace a gun Charvat had taken from back of the bar, according to Lt. Lester Connerty, head of the Cicero detective bureau.

Instead of returning the weapon to its place behind the bar, Charvat gave it to Miss Wakefield, who then shot the Chicagoan in the right leg, according to police.

Thursday Barbara Wakefield told Judge E. Marvin Capouch that Jarecki had lunged at her and she had shot in self defense.

Howard Risk, 1553 S. Central Park ave., Chicago, who said he had witnessed the shooting, told the court that he snatched the gun away from Miss Wakefield after she shot Jarecki for no apparent reason.

A second shot was fired but went wild when Risk attempted to take the .32 caliber automatic away from Barbara Wakefield, according to Lt. Connerty.

The shooting took place when Jarecki and Charvat went outside to discuss their differences after Jarecki had lost his money in a dice game, according to testimony in court Thursday.

Wally went outside with the gang following him. Then DJ told Wally to give the gun to his girlfriend. As soon as she got the gun, she started blasting away at the bikers and hit DJ in the leg. I cursed her and grabbed the gun. An ambulance came and took DJ to the hospital. The police arrived and took Wally's girlfriend into custody.

In time, the case went to court. I was living in Los Angeles at the time and received a small check from DJ for my part in the shooting. The police tried again and again to close down Wally and Genes, but to no avail. One of the cops even went so far as to send his teenage daughter to order drinks.

The one thought that comes to mind when I think of Roy's, another bike hangout, is an embarrassment to me. The previous night, a couple of us were riding through the streets when we saw flashing lights behind us. Without thinking, we took evasive action and sped away from the lights. We managed to get away after about ten minutes of maneuvering through traffic up and down Harlem Avenue and in and out of side streets. The next night at Roy's, when I had a good-size audience, I proceeded to brag about how we outran the cops. I had everyone's attention and thought why the gang was paying such strict attention to my story. Then I turned around and saw the officer who had chased us. There was only one officer on duty that night, and he was it. Today I still feel very embarrassed when I think of that incident.

There were nights when everything was just right. The weather, the moon, our attitude toward one another, and someone would say, "Lets go to Joliet." And we would be off on a bike ride to Joliet for a hamburger or a cup of coffee.

Bull was a McCook cop who used to be a bike rider. He seemed to hold it against bike riders when they came through McCook. I was stopped once. Bull jumped out of his police car and took out his gun and threatened to put a bullet up my ass. He screamed for my driver's license. I showed it to him. He found many things wrong with my bike and ticketed me, all the time screaming and cursing at me. He finally let me go. After I came to California, someone sent me a clipping from the newspaper that stated that Bull had a prisoner in the McCook Police Station, and while Bull went for a drink, the prisoner snuck up on Bull and removed his gun and shot and killed him.

Now Schultz's name was not Schultz but Byrnes or Burns. Anyway Schultz went on a job interview. The interviewer called him in by spelling his name. He kept getting it wrong so Schultz stood up and said, "Look, just call me Schultz." The name stuck and from that day on, his name was Schultz. Schultz didn't have a bike, so I would pick him up and take him with me to all the bike hangouts. He was worth having around because he was entertaining. All the girls liked him, which didn't hurt my status in the gang.

Tiger was the only gal that rode solo and hung out with the guys in all of the bike hangouts. She drank her share of beer and was officially one of the guys although she didn't have to be told that. Tiger was an institution among motorcycle riders all over the city. We all had our accidents while riding our bikes, including Tiger.

One warm and balmy night, the kind that bike riders like, I rode my bike into Lemont to pick up tamales. I got the tamales, put them in a bag in my left hand, and, with my right hand, steered my way out of town on a four-lane road when suddenly the four-lane road turned into a two-lane road. I swerved to get back on the road but hit a huge hole. I flew over the handlebars and landed on my back on the ground. My bike landed on top of me and cut off my breathing. The bike's engine started up and made a terrific noise. Some farmers heard the noise and ran and took the bike off of me. An ambulance came and took me to St. Joseph's Hospital in Joliet where my doctor put a cast from my neck to my midsection and another on my right arm. I was in the hospital for three weeks and in the cast for six months, I went to the doctor for therapy and, in time, the casts were taken off. I thank you, Dr. Blondis, for taking good care of me. My arm was very functional after I completed therapy, and I've never had a bit of trouble with it since. I don't know what happened to my bike, but to continue riding would have killed my mother.

Monk rode with his mother on the back of his bike. I'll always remember Monk's laughter and carefree attitude. In time, it became known that he was having an affair with his mother. How does that sit with you? It was one of those things that you never think about. Anyway, Monk knew it was wrong, and she knew it was wrong, and God knew it was wrong. So Monk took a gun, put it to his head, and committed suicide. I can't even imagine the frame of mind he was in when he pulled the trigger.

PART THREE

THE AIR FORCE

It was 1950, and the Korean War was on. I never gave it much thought except that I might get called up, so for some unknown reason, I got a car and drove to Los Angeles. There was an ad in the *Chicago Tribune* that needed a driver to bring a car to Los Angeles from Chicago. I applied and got the job. I had ten days to drive two thousand miles on the famous Route 66, which was made famous by the Nat "King" Cole hit "Route 66." My eyes saw things they were not used to seeing; the southwest desert, the Grand Canyon, two-lane highways that made a straight line across the dry desert, real cowboys, and signs that read: "Rip a Fender off Your Car, Send It in for a Half-pound Jar, Burma Shave," "Last Stop for Gas," "See the Three-headed Cow," "Real Live Dinosaur Next Gas Stop," "Gas—25 Cents," "See the Petrified Forest," "See the Half Jackrabbit, Half Mule Next Gas Stop." I drove off of the highway in Arizona and got stuck in soft sand at about four o'clock in the afternoon. I did everything I could to get free. About ten o'clock the next morning, a trucker saw my predicament and pulled me back onto the road with heavy-duty ropes he had on his rig. All he wanted for helping me out was a glass of wine and a raw egg. I met him at the next town and gladly paid him for his help.

I pulled into a gas station in Arizona and emptied my radiator of water and put in fresh water. An indignant proprietor ran over to inform me that he paid a quarter per gallon for water and not to waste any of it.

I finally made it to California and stayed with my cousins up on Beachwood Drive in Hollywood. Cousin Mike had gone through World War II and had seen a lot of action, but he never talked about it. One of my cousin's friends, Bob Press, and I agreed to join the air force together. We got up early one morning and took the bus to Olympic Boulevard in downtown Los Angeles where we were sworn in. Our plan was to stay together while in the air force, but the military had different ideas and separated us that very day. That was the last time we saw each other for forty years. We had a lot of catching up to do once we were reunited.

I eventually wound up at Kindley Air Force Base in Bermuda where I was assigned to a Hurricane Hunter outfit. All of the time, I was having migraine headaches and fits of depression. I went on sick call regularly.

I was given a rifle and told to guard a prisoner. It was made clear that he could go anywhere on base: to get his mail, to the latrine, to the barracks, to the PX, and any reasonable place on the base. But if he were to attempt to escape, I was to shoot him. I talked to the prisoner and told him the rules. I looked him seriously in the eye and told him that I was from Chicago and that I wouldn't hesitate to shoot him if he tried to escape. I'm glad we had that little talk. He was no trouble for the rest of the day, and when the day was finished, I was glad to get rid of my gun and hand him over to the MPs. If he had tried to escape, I wouldn't have shot him.

Another gun incident was when I was given a rifle and told to guard a munitions depot with another airman. It was a pitch-black midnight, and we were driven to the location where the munitions were. We were to march back and forth and challenge anyone who approached us. He was to walk from one end of the compound, and I from the other. We met in the middle and reversed our steps, turned around, and walked back to our starting point. We were both brand-new airmen and did only what we were told to do. That was a memorable, miserable air force experience.

I was an usher at the Lackland Air Force Base Theater on Thanksgiving Day in 1950. At dinnertime, I become quite hungry, especially when I heard an NCO talking about how delicious his Thanksgiving meal was. I mustered enough nerve to go to him and ask when I could get my Thanksgiving dinner. I mentioned to him that the theater was completely empty. He looked at the other NCO and said, "What do you think, should we let him go?" There was a long silence and then, "Okay, go ahead." It was way past dinnertime, but it was Thanksgiving. I ran to an empty mess hall and asked the cook for my Thanksgiving meal. He told me that the turkey was all gone but there might be some scraps left. That was it. All because two inconsiderate NCOs had their fill of food but were not willing to let anyone else have theirs. That was my introduction into the air force. I've never forgotten that. I didn't say anything because I was a brand-new airman and afraid of my shadow.

My spiritual life was okay, but I never wanted to stop learning about the God of the Bible, so I continued studying. Now my headaches were getting worse, and the military doctors were baffled as to what it might be. One doctor said that if the headaches persisted, he thought I should submit myself to a frontal lobotomy. That had me worried.

To get the military to take you seriously, one had to repeatedly go on sick call. I did. I was hospitalized and took many tests to help the doctors make a diagnosis. There was the Rorschach or inkblot test, then redrawing a simple picture that had been shown you, then a battery of tests to conclude what job you were best suited for in the Air Force. Three times mine came out music, art, and literature. I was so tense during the picture-copying test that I broke the lead in the pencil several times and perspired heavily.

Eventually, as a patient, I was sent to Wright-Patterson Air Force Base in Ohio via ambulance. The driver of the ambulance pulled up to the hospital, which was temporary, I'm sure. We walked up the wooden stairs and entered. I held on to my duffle bag and followed the driver down a long narrow hall. We came around one corner, and I saw a hand-painted sign hanging from the ceiling. It read, "Mental Hygiene." We entered an open double door and proceeded to walk a few feet until we entered a hospital ward. Smitty, the ward orderly, greeted us as we entered. The driver handed Smitty my papers, waited for a signature, and left. Smitty shook my hand and said if I hurried, I could make it to chow. He showed me how to get to the mess hall. I hurried and ate dinner and returned to the ward where several of the other patients in the ward had gathered after chow.

Smitty was off duty when I returned. The new orderly was a female black captain. She called me into her room and introduced herself. She told me that every morning, Captain Guzvich, our psychiatrist, made the rounds with several of his staff to see how the patients were doing. One of the staff took notes as the patient's relayed information to the doctor on how they were doing.

The doctor told me to come to his office as soon as his rounds were over. He asked me how I was feeling, what my sleep patterns were like, when did I get my headaches, whether I wanted out of the service, and a lot of questions about myself. He said I could go to town anytime I wanted, but he would expect me to be at my bunk in the morning when he made his rounds. That was the beginning of a very interesting time in my life. For the next three months, I came in contact with every type of personality: the mean and vicious, the over exuberant, the extreme pessimist, the delusional, the depressed and sad, crybabies, and those who appeared normal. I was beginning to gain insight into some of the other patients' idiosyncrasies. It was easy to see their faults and not my own. But isn't that always the case? There were those who were absolute loners and wanted nothing to do with anyone, not even Dr. Guzvich.

An example of a delusional patient was the airman who bunked next to me. He was a Hispanic from Texas, who could be seen at any hour of the day or night sitting on the edge of his bunk staring into space. He was constantly listening to the voice of his mother arguing with members of his family. "There they go again," he would say to me. We spoke casually until the voices came back. He was considered incompetent and was allowed only two dollars a month from his pay. I would give him a couple of dollars from time to time.

Although there were little clicks in the ward, I got to know most of the other patients and their habits. Unexpected incidents occurred from time to time, like the time Saffold offered me ten dollars if I would get a rope for him to hang himself. More about that later.

The main reasons for my being in a mental hygiene ward were my migraines and extreme bouts of depression. I didn't miss a single morning when Dr. Guzvich made his rounds. I slowly fitted into my place. I saw patients come and go. Dr. Guzvich kept patients long enough to fairly evaluate them and to recommend to a board whether or not that particular airman should be honorably discharged or serve out the rest of their time in the air force.

We had an airman who had been a mortician in civilian life, a racehorse breeder, a professional air force major, a mechanic, several noncoms, and a bunch of guys who thought that living the air force life was the greatest, and for them it was. As I got to know them on a personal level, I became more aware why some of them were committed to a mental hygiene ward and was also aware that some of them were perpetrating a facade in order to get out of the service.

Up to the time when the horse breeder went home on a three-day pass, he sounded and acted perfectly normal. But when he staggered into the ward two days later with shirt hanging out of his pants, completely disoriented, swearing, and coughing hard, Dr. Guzvich came out of his office. The horse breeder took a swing at the doctor and missed. His pants dropped to his ankles, and he tripped over them and fell to the floor flat on his face. He gasped for breath. Dr. Guzvich ordered Smitty to run and get some oxygen. He applied the oxygen and put the horse breeder to bed. When the horse breeder woke up, he explained how he and his brother had strong differences on how to manage their ranch. The horse breeder was frustrated and went out and got drunk.

Right after payday, the mortician went to town with another airman to get drunk. He was picked up by the Military Police and returned to the hospital in cuffs. The nurse in charge tried to have him released to her custody. The MPs were crude and arrogant and said no way. She got on the phone to the base commander who hurried to the ward in his pajamas. The nurse introduced him to the MPs who by now were standing at attention. She told the base commander about the incident with the MPs. The base commander ordered the MPs to take the cuffs off of the mortician. He then did something that touched me. He bent over the mortician, touched his cheek, and softly asked, "Are you alright, son?" Then he turned angrily toward the MPs and said, "You bastards. Can't you tell when a man is hurting? Now you get your asses out of here right now. And I don't want to hear about you harassing the men in this ward, or I'll hang you. Understand? Now git out!"

Ruth Klein was in charge of the Red Cross at the base hospital. She gave strict orders that the girls that volunteered for the Red Cross were not to date any of the patients. One of the patients made a date with one of the girls but never showed up. The girl blamed Ruth. Ruth took the girl back to the mental hygiene ward and showed her the patient that she was to have the date with. He was sitting in front of the TV, staring straight ahead. Ruth called out his name. He did not respond. The point was made.

We could make anything we wanted at the Red Cross: silver earrings, necklaces, and watchbands. Ruth was trying to help one of the patients from my ward when he exploded and told her to mind her own business. Incidents like these were reported to Dr. Guzvich to assist in evaluating the patient.

Across a grassy knoll was another ward, a closed ward with bars on the windows and the entryway. You could gain entrance from the hallway or look into their windows across the knoll. I was in my ward near a window and heard someone call out to me. "Hey, man. Over here, man." I looked out the window and saw a set of windows. I vaguely saw a figure at the window. I knew that this was the airman who called out to me. We carried on a conversation, not only that day, but many days that followed. We talked about why each of us had joined the Air Force, where we were from, the food in the mess hall, authority, and a host of other things. One day, I went to the window expecting to see him, but I saw nothing. I never saw him again.

He had completely disappeared. Finally, I went to the entrance of the closed ward and knocked on the door. A nurse came and unlocked the door. I told her I was in the open ward next door and asked if she knew anything about the airman who I had been communicating with through the window. She looked perplexed but asked me to follow her. She showed me an empty area near the window. I could feel her eyes on me. She assured me that no patient came to that window and carried on a conversation with anyone in the next ward. I didn't argue the point. She was an officer. I went back to my ward completely confused, wondering. I didn't say anything to anyone about the incident, but I kept going back to the window, hoping that I would see him again. I never did. Was I hallucinating? I'm sure that the nurse reported the incident to Dr. Guzvich.

When I couldn't sleep, I would pace back and forth. The nurse on duty invited me into her office. We chatted about various things. One of which was an officer who had seen much military action but now was admitted to a mental hygiene ward of a military hospital for observation. Whenever he got near the Capitol building in Washington DC, he saw John Foster Dulles sitting on the dome of the Capitol. Not just once, but whenever he got near the Capitol. He had no other manifestations of mental illness, just that one thing.

A young fighter pilot who returned from the war was found standing in the rain, in uniform, at night, staring into a downtown store window for hours, crying, until the MPs found him and took him back to the base.

There were a few airmen in the ward who appeared perfectly normal until you spent time with them. One patient walked around all day with a smile on his face. He would walk from the Red Cross to the ward and back to the Red Cross, always smiling but never saying anything. When he got back to his bunk, he would straighten his blanket and pillow and off he would go again. Or McFadden, who had no respect for anyone or anything and who constantly argued with the doctors and everyone in the ward about everything.

There was a young Air Force wife hospitalized in a room next to our ward. Her husband was in combat, and the thought of him dying got to her. Sometimes she laughed, but most of the time, she sat on the edge of her bed crying. There was an Air Force nurse in the room who took care of her.

The mortician closed the door to the game room and sat down inside at the piano. He should have been a concert pianist. He mesmerized the rest of us with his artistry. Another time, he went into the sound room in the hospital and played record after record for the patients and staff. No one objected to his playing.

A Yemeni was in the ward with the rest of us. How he ever got into the service is beyond me. He went by his rules and only by his rules. But because we were both originally from the Middle East, we hung out together at times. I had to explain to the nurses that that's the way people from Yemen were. I went home to Chicago on a three-day pass, and he decided to tag along, with the understanding that I was to visit my relatives when we got to Chicago with no interruptions from him. As we went through small towns on the way, he would make calls to synagogues and churches before he got to that particular town and tell them that he was in the service and that he needed a place to stay for the night. He usually wound up with a place to stay and a few dollars, when a few dollars meant something. He was a quick talker, very outgoing, and fearless.

Nobody liked Saffold, and he didn't like any of us. He was arrogant, brash, and mean; so when he was scheduled to go before the board, we all crossed our fingers that he would get booted out of the service or sent back to duty. The day that he was to go before the board, I walked into the latrine and found him leaning against the wall in the corner in suntans. He said to me, "Hey, man. You wanna make ten bucks? Get me a rope." I immediately thought this guy wanted to commit suicide. I walked all over the hospital looking for a rope but didn't find one. Then I remembered that they had lamps in the Red Cross with sashes on them. I went to the Red Cross and pulled a sash from one of the lamps and took it to Saffold. I didn't wait for my ten dollars. Then I went back to my ward and laid down in my bunk. Four hours later, I got up and went to Smitty and told him about Saffold and him wanting a rope. I told Smitty that I thought Saffold wanted to kill himself. Smitty immediately called Dr. Guzvich who came running. They found Saffold lying outside on the grass unconscious. The sash didn't work, so he swallowed a handful of pills and lived. Dr. Guzvich had Saffold's stomach pumped. No one ever brought up the incident to me. As far as I was concerned, it never happened, but I'm sure it went on my medical record.

I was walking between buildings on the base and saw one of the guys from the ward walking toward me holding two paper bags. He was glassy eyed and stared beyond me. The bottom of one bag was wet, and a bottle was about to fall out of it. I approached him, but he didn't recognize me. All he said was "I hit her. I hit her." After a while, I took him by the arm and led him back to the ward. A bottle of whiskey fell out of the bottom of one bag. Both bags were full of liquor. I don't know how he managed to get two bags full of liquor into the base and in his hospital clothes. He told me that he was driving his car downtown and that he hit a pregnant woman. Dr. Guzvich looked into the matter and found out there was no report of a pregnant woman in town hit by a car. This airman had seen action in two wars, and my opinion was that stress had finally gotten to him. This kind of situation was not unusual for the patients in my ward.

I was a patient in the hospital for about three months. At first, you're the new guy on the block, and you must earn the right to hang out with certain people. After a while, you develop friendships with certain other patients that you have something in common with. It takes approximately three months for a good therapist to observe and evaluate you. The staff was great, but I don't remember any incident with other patients that stand out. I had some friends while I was a patient, but none that I could remember. I still didn't trust people to get that close to me and have never felt that close to anyone, man or woman.

I was adjusting well to hospital life, except I still had headaches. Every morning, Dr. Guzvich would make his rounds; and every day, there was someone who had an imaginary or real illness. On weekends, I usually hitchhiked home for two days and stayed at my Aunt Vicki's house. I was more comfortable with her than with my mother. I still had strong feelings of being rejected by her. At times, these feelings took over, and I would get all tensed up and totally exhausted, and it was at these times that I felt like running and jumping through a plate glass window.

If I allowed myself the luxury of thinking about bad thoughts, it was usually at a time when I had to make a decision about something and just couldn't decide, like the time I started for home and got as far as town. I decided to go back to the base. But if I stayed on the base, I would be lonely. So I decided not to stay but to go home. No, I would stay on the base . . . but I . . . another drink would do it . . . . and a third. Then I took the bus back to the base and staggered into the ward, crying and looking for Dr. Guzvich. He was nowhere to be found. He usually was not available on weekends. I didn't have good feelings for him then. I expected him to be there when I needed him.

A drunken patient staggered into Dr. Guzvich's office and cupped his hands in front of the doctor. "What's that," the doctor asked. "That's my life, and I don't want it." Dr. Guzvich saw an opportunity and grabbed it. "What do you mean you don't want it? You're stuck with it." "What if I told you something I never told anyone else." "Go ahead," the doctor replied. The patient threw his head back, bit his finger, and started saying, "Nobody . . . ever . . . told me . . . nobody . . . ever . . . told . . . me they loved me." Dr. Guzvich said, "It's all right to cry." The patient shook his head no. After two long minutes, he burst out crying and fell to the floor. A nurse opened the door and asked, "Is everything all right in here?" Dr. Guzvich threw a book at her and very angrily yelled, "Get out. Get out now."

After I received an honorable discharge from the air force, I went to Los Angeles and turned myself over to the Veterans Administration for therapy. I was in therapy for one and a half years, twice a week. I never missed a session. For one and a half years, I talked about my childhood, my current lifestyle, my sex life, my relationship with my grandparents and my mother, my spiritual life, my current feelings about dating, my spells of loneliness, my headaches and depression, and anything that was in my heart. During that time, I experienced extreme periods of rejection by girls I was going out with. Not that they rejected me, but I feared that they might reject me. Two and two were suddenly coming together to equal four. One experience related to another and another and another. I was beginning to see light. On my last session, I was told that I now had tools to work with and that I should use these tools, and yes, I could come back if I ever felt that I needed additional therapy. I came back once, I believe, just to test the system. I haven't had a headache in over forty years, and I can handle depression. I can accept women in my life without my heart racing a mile a minute and without breaking out in a sweat and my throat drying up. I've become a flirt, and I love it—all of it. Yes, I've done a complete hundred-and-eighty-degree turnaround.

PART FOUR

SYNANON

I understand that the word *synanon* came out of the meaning of the word *seminar*. A group of drug addicts and alcoholics got together in a basement somewhere to express themselves and try to get cured when one of them uttered the word *synanon* instead of the word *seminar*. They thought of having *synanons* (seminars) and talk their way out of their addiction. That's my understanding. Chuck Dederich, Sr. was the founder of Synanon. Anyway, many years ago, I read about Synanon and felt obligated to go to Santa Monica and offer my help. I went to the beach in search of their building and found it. I went in and saw a girl behind a desk and identified myself and told her why I was there. She rang a buzzer, and an older man came from upstairs and invited me to have coffee and donuts. We talked, and I was invited to come back Saturday when they would have open houses. I became a regular and eventually I earned the right to take some of the residents to town for coffee and a sandwich.

Most of the residents were hardcore drug addicts or alcoholics who turned themselves over to Synanon for a cure. In time, they had a chartered company and a cattle ranch and many other enterprises to keep money flowing into the institution and to keep themselves busy because idle hands have a habit of getting into trouble. Their rent and food bill must have been astronomical. Donations came in huge denominations. People who were in favor of Synanon had given clothing, food, furniture, and free legal advice. But those who were opposed to "dope fiends" in their midst did everything they could to make life miserable for Synanon residents. But in time, Synanon grew and grew until sociologists began making studies and writing papers about the institution.

If you were a person addicted to drugs or liquor and you wanted to be free of your habit, you might want to go to Synanon and turn yourself over to them. At first, you'd be given very menial chores to perform, such as cleaning toilets or scrubbing floors. There were two rules that you had to abide by: no drugs or alcohol on the property and no fighting. Everyone leaned on one another.

I can give a thumbnail sketch of what happens when someone splits. I got to know Danny quite well. He was a hardcore drug user from New York, who came out to the West Coast to turn himself over to Synanon. The word had gotten out about Synanon in the world of illegal drug users. I would see Danny at the Saturday open houses. We became quite close. Then for some reason, the regimentation got to him, and he split. The first thing he did was to contact me. He began borrowing money from me, two dollars at a time. But he always paid me back when he said he would. I don't know where he was staying. His mom sent him money for rent. He said he was drug free, but everyone at Synanon knows that once you're a user, the chances are you might go back to the habit. For some reason, Danny didn't have much of a life and decided to go back to Synanon. Here's where it gets interesting. When I left him in Synanon, I knew that there was more to him just being accepted back into the fold. First, the secretary called upstairs and told the higher-ups that Danny was back. They made him wait for more than five hours before anyone could talk to him. The other residents were told not to speak a word to him if they saw him waiting. He had to get permission to take a drink of water or go to the bathroom, and he had nothing to eat. They were doing their best to humble him and to see how badly he wanted back. Finally, they called him in and had him tell his story. For starters, they took away his false teeth and gave him baggy trousers that were twenty inches too big around the waist, shoes that were several sizes too large, and a hat with a long feather sticking out on the top of it. But the worse part of it was a sign that they hung around his neck stating that he was to be treated like a little boy and that he was dumb and stupid and had other insulting comments. Because he wanted to get out of the building and get some fresh air, he had to mingle with the Sunday crowd on the beach in Santa Monica in his Synanon clothes.

The next time he split was for good when his mother came out from New York. She adored Danny and had to be near him. Ethyl was a Russian Jewess, and he was her kinf. They both wanted to tell me his story, so they sat with me and gave me eleven hours of revealing testimony. I thought I might be able to do something with it commercially. Ethyl explained how Danny hurt his back working in New York. The doctors gave him drugs for the pain until one day the doctors weren't around, and Danny thought he would die from the pain. His friends told him where he could get some drugs on the street. Danny began buying until he realized he was a user. He stole, he lied, he cheated, and he did everything and anything to get money for drugs. He got most of his drugs from pharmacists who sold to drug addicts illegally. Sometimes an addict would get hold of a prescription pad, and they would write their own prescriptions. Danny once told me that sophisticated drug addicts know how to write a prescription better than most doctors and which drugs are the best.

Danny came pounding on my door about 2:00 a.m. He pushed his way into my apartment and insisted that I give him ten bucks. I knew that he had fallen off the wagon and needed to score. I sat him down. "I'll never use again, man. Honest." I knew that he was lying. I stalled for time. He started to go to sleep; then all of a sudden, he was wide-awake. He started pacing back and forth, and then he sat down for a short while. "Man, you don't understand. I need ten dollars, man." Two hours after Danny arrived at my place, I called Pam, a mutual friend, and told her the story. She said to come over right away. I got Danny in my car and was driving to Pam's when Danny saw an all-night service station. He yelled for me to stop; then he jumped out of the car and ran inside the service station and grabbed the attendant by the neck. "Give me your money, man." I grabbed Danny and dragged him to the car and drove the rest of the way to Pam's. She let us in and began sweet-talking Danny. His whole attitude changed, and he curled up on the sofa and slept for a couple of hours. When he woke up, he was his old self again.

There were residents at Synanon with a five-hundred-dollars-a-day habit. Danny's habit was a lot less expensive, but nevertheless, he had to rob someone to get the money for his next fix. Sometimes he would take money from his mother's purse without her knowledge. He would get in line in an alley behind a pharmacy to get his illegal fix from the pharmacist. In the same line were debutantes, lawyers, laborers, engineers, and students. Ethyl threatened the pharmacists and said she was going to report them to the police, but Danny begged her not to do it because he needed just one more shot. Ethyl cried when she saw Danny that way. I tried to get emotion out of her when taping their story and would say something like, "Ethyl, why do you put up with his shit? He's a dope fiend." She would get angry and cry and clutch her breast and say, "Whatta ya talking? He's mine kinf." Then she would look up at God and say," Please, God, I'm begging you. Let him be all right." She called me her other son and that God should be good to me. When she didn't know what to do, she would read her Bible and cry. I've never seen a mother that had as much devotion to her child as she had for Danny. There were cops selling drugs to users on the street corner. Ethyl would plead for them to stop selling that stuff, but Danny would finally win out by telling Ethyl that he needed just one more shot and not to turn the policeman in.

I met Gary at a church in downtown Los Angeles. The preacher asked for prayers for a young man who had to go to court in Las Vegas for possession of marijuana. I met the man later, and we began hanging out together. He had a wife and an adorable little girl. The Las Vegas court wanted to see him quite often and demanded that he return to Vegas. His case kept being postponed until one day he was sentenced from ten to twenty years for possession of marijuana. Nobody believed it. But they did have a billboard on The Strip that explained the harsh penalties for drug users. He was allowed only four or five people to correspond with per month. I was one of those. The prison system in Nevada was using the Synanon program for addicts. After seven years, Gary was released. Before Gary went to prison, he was a top jazz drummer in the country. He continued being a drummer in prison. But now that he was out of the joint, jobs were hard to come by. We hung around for a while after he got out; then we lost track of each other.

PART FIVE

PHOTOGRAPHY

I was walking down Hollywood Boulevard and met a friend, Dora, from church. I told her I was looking for a job. She suggested that I go to Capitol Records and apply in the photo studio because she was aware that I had a background in photography. I talked to the supervisor in the photo studio at Capitol, and he hired me to come in and work a few hours a day in the darkroom printing black-and-white pictures of Capitol artists. After a few months, I was hired full-time.

I was still doing darkroom printing, but now I was also taking pictures of Capitol artists, going to clubs at night to shoot an artist's opening and shooting publicity photos for our files. I was making a name for myself in Hollywood.

At times, I was given an assignment and was more interested in the final photo results than the artist. Many years later, I was contacted by an agency who wanted to buy me out. Why would anyone want my photos? When I finally examined my library of negatives, I realized that I had photographed quite a few top celebrities: Bob Hope, Sonny and Cher, Crosby, Stills, and Nash, the Rolling Stones, Rod Stewart, Jimmie Durante, Ira Gershwin, the Beatles, the Beach Boys, Wayne Newton, David Rose, the Monkees, Kay Starr, Merle Haggard, Nat "King" Cole, *The Johnny Carson Show*, the Academy Awards, the Rose Parade, and many others. Once you work for Capitol, your name gets around town, and you're in demand.

My camera soon became a part of me, and I had it with me wherever I went. Gals that I had worked with at Capitol, who now worked at other recording companies, often called to give me work. I would shoot club openings, publicity photos, album covers, and magazine spreads, so I had to be ready at any time. I was given assignments out of town and had to pack my bags and cameras and be on a plane within a few hours.

After a while, I began freelancing. The bad part of that was getting paid. I wasn't a businessman, so I had some contracts printed up with every little detail spelled out: date of shooting, time to arrive, how long I was to work, name of person hiring me and their signature, price to be paid, when I was to be paid, what size photos the customer was to get, and all the other business considerations. No more doing business with just a handshake.

Like so many actors and musicians, Ira and George Gershwin were raised in New York's lower east side of Manhattan. Ira took me on a tour of his fabulous Beverly Hills home before his death and mesmerized me with tales about him and his brother George. I was in his home to shoot publicity photos of an up-and-coming teenage pianist with Ira Gershwin. I shot against a huge mural that was on the wall showing a theater from the viewpoint of a person on stage and the balcony and ground floor of the theater. I think he said it was a mural of his brother George on stage. That was the most memorable background that I shot that day. Undoubtedly, these two brothers, Ira and George, were the greatest songwriter team in history. Ira wrote the lyrics, and George wrote the music. There was a rumor that Ira depended entirely on his brother's talents. Nonsense. Ira was an artist in his own right.

I had an assignment to shoot Jimmie Durante the following week after the shoot in Mr. Gershwin's home, so I thought I would kill two birds with one stone and get the Durante shooting while I was that close to him. After all, he lived right up the street from Mr. Gershwin's home. I knocked on the door, and Mr. Durante answered. I told him the story, and as usual, he was very helpful. The people who hired me not only wanted photos of Mr. Durante, but also wanted me to ask him for an identifiable item that was associated with him that might be auctioned. He thought for a while and came up with a great idea, his hat, which was his trademark. He took it off and gave it to me, and I turned it over to my people. His mother could be credited for his large nose, which incidentally has been preserved in cement at Grauman's Chinese Theatre.

Shooting Sonny and Cher's first concert at the Hollywood Bowl was a novelty. When they appeared on stage, I knew immediately that they were the main act of the night. Cher was just nineteen and became scared when some of the kids climbed up on stage to remove the decorations on her toreador pants as souvenirs. She took the mike and tearfully begged the kids to cool it. She said that she was scared. The kids obliged and backed off. Sonny and Cher found fame with "I Got You Babe." Prior to this, they billed themselves as Caesar and Cleo. Sonny died in a ski accident in 1998.

Kay Starr

It was time for Kay Starr to do another album. I was to shoot the publicity photos. She took a break and laid her reading glasses on her sheet music with her name prominent under the title of the song. I saw photographic potential and spent the next fifteen minutes shooting the arrangement. Of course, I shot photos of Kay to show that she was in a recording session. Between 1948 and 1954, she had a string of hits.

The day Nat "King" Cole died was a sad day for the world of music. Capitol closed down for the day. In the photo studio, we paid homage to Nat by placing a director's chair in the middle of the studio with a spotlight on it and the shades drawn. A TV news crew picked up on it and showed it on the six o'clock news. How I remember "Straighten Up and Fly Right," "Sweet Lorraine," and "Nature Boy."

"The greatest thing you'll ever learn is just to love and be loved in return."

Milt Raskin, music composer and arranger, came up to the photo studio to ask me to shoot his upcoming wedding to Margie, which took place in Hidden Valley in the hills off of Mulholland in the home of Bob whatzisname, guitar player in the Johnny Carson big band conducted by Doc Severenson. Johnny Mercer, George Shearing, and other celebrities were there. Milt told me to shoot in black and white. I've always wanted to shoot a wedding in black and white. The invited musicians brought their horns, so after a while, we had a jam session with Johnny Mercer on vocals and George Shearing on the piano. I stayed half the night. Shearing was born in London, blind at age three. When he came to America, he joined the jazz scene playing for such greats as Peggy Lee and Mel Torme. Johnny Mercer collaborated with "Duke" Ellington and Hoagy Carmichael and wrote music and lyrics for such hits as "I'm an Old Cow Hand," "GI Jive," and "Moon River" from the movie *Breakfast at Tiffany's*, and so many more huge hits.

I was shooting David Rose for an album cover while he was conducting in a Capitol recording studio when he asked me to wait until he got a haircut. I already had my pictures of him, so I stayed around to talk to him about his hobby—trains. Not the kind of trains you build in your spare room, but an elaborate set of trains that you build in your backyard that real live people could ride on.

I was approached by a tabloid editor about shooting for his paper. I was told I could make a lot of money for the right pictures by situating myself on a rooftop across the street from a hospital and getting pictures of actresses leaving the hospital with their newborn babies. The pay was astronomical, but I declined.

I was called to the Marriott Hotel on Century Boulevard to shoot Governor Ronald Reagan with the maitre d' of the hotel. I identified myself and was led into a room to wait. Meanwhile, I was given a little fold-over pin to put on my lapel, which identified me as one of the good guys. After a short while, I was asked to go into the room where the governor and the maitre d' were in. One of the Secret Service agents who escorted me noticed that my pin was not attached to my lapel. I had lost it. We both got on our hands and knees and rubbed our open hands over the carpet. He found it and firmly put it back on me. I got to the room where the governor and the maitre d' were in and took the photos. This was one of two times that I had met Mr. Reagan. He was a true gentleman.

I left the hotel and went outside to shoot the governor in his car as he left the hotel. There were wooden barricades set up to keep the people back. I set up on the side with the news photographers. A photographer jumped over the barricades and positioned himself right in front of me so that I couldn't see a thing. I jumped over the barricade and got in front of him. While we were vying for the best positions, the cars with the governor and his retinue exited onto Century Boulevard. Neither of us got a formal picture.

Judy Garland was in the smaller recording studio at Capitol as I was leaving. She was with Vic Damone. I thought I would ask her for a photo, but no sooner had I entered the studio than one of the Capitol employees approached me and said that Mrs. Garland would like me to leave. No problem. I left.

Ken Kim, a local art director, had an assignment to shoot "Count" Basie, but he had another assignment and couldn't make it, so he asked me to shoot the "Count". I've always appreciated "Count" Basie's music, and I was delighted that I was able to shoot him and listen to his great sound. I got great shots of him writing music and conferring with the producer of the album. They used a lot of my shots on the album.

I did quite a few sessions with Bill Bixby of *The Magician*, his current TV series. I arrived on the set and was told he might be in his dressing room. I knocked and entered. He was pouring wine for himself and his wife. It was lunchtime for them. He invited me to pull up a chair and join them. Of course, I declined. I knew that he didn't have much time with his wife while working on his series. I waited until he had a break and took the pictures. I thought it was very nice of him to offer me lunch.

I knew Jane Russell and her family, and I hung out with two of her brothers, Jamie and Tom. I guess word got around that I knew her. I began getting calls from producers who wanted her to appear on TV or to make guest appearances. I always said no to these people. It would have violated her trust. Jane was quite feisty at times, but no more so than any one else.

Someone at Capitol signed Mae West to do an album. She came up to the photo studio with a huge entourage of people: a hairdresser, a makeup artist, a wardrobe mistress, and a lot of other people. I don't believe the album ever took off. She was eighty years old at the time and an institution. She was very particular who took her pictures, so everyone backed off, except the photo lab supervisor.

I went to the Greek Theater in the Hollywood Hills to shoot Crosby, Stills, and Nash. During a break, one of them took the mike and in effect announced to the audience that the recent walk on the moon by our astronauts was phony journalism and that the event never took place. This showed ignorance on his part. When it was proved that the event actually did happen, his mouth would be shut forever. It's better to be quiet and thought dumb than to speak and remove all doubt.

"Green-eyed Lady" was a big hit for Sugarloaf, the band. I got a call to go to Denver and get some publicity photos of them. It was winter, and it was cold and dreary. I wasn't happy with the shoot and neither was the art director, so we had them come to Los Angeles, where I knew the town well enough to have a list of thirty or more location spots. We went to a deserted house on Highland in Hollywood where we spent some time, and then we wound up in Griffith Park. I was getting warmer now. I could feel good things happening photographically. I did some photographic trickery and got an exploded photo of them. The art director and I sandwiched two negatives together and came up with a great shot for the liner using the exploded shot. The art director was happy, and I was happy, and of course, Sugarloaf was happy.

I spent three days in Vegas taking photos of Sergio Franchi at his home and also on stage while performing in a club at night. He was very personable. I also took some great photos of his beautiful daughter. I felt privileged to be the only photographer allowed in the club while he was performing. I didn't do as well with a group called Carnival. I went to Vegas to take publicity photos of them. When one of the girls found out that I took a room at the same hotel that they were in, she made comments to the effect that I was interested in getting to know her better and wanted to be close to her. Absolutely not. That ruined my photographic efforts. The photos could have been better. There was a carnival in town, so I posed them in front of it and got some acceptable photos.

Mrs. Miller was an off-key singer, way off-key. I never did find out whether or not she knew that she couldn't carry a tune in a bucket, but I liked her. Since her album had a country flavor, I headed for the stables in Glendale on Riverside Drive. As luck would have it, it rained and rained. The next day, it rained again, so I gave up and went back to the studio at Capitol. I had rented her a Western outfit and a guitar and shot the photos in the studio for the album cover. I finally got my photos for the cover, but only after rearranging my plans several times.

SUSIE

My next assignment was to shoot LSD parties on the Sunset Strip for an album that Capitol was producing. I met Larry Schiller, the producer, at midnight, and we headed to our first party. I got along well with the kids because I think I have a lot of street savvy. After two or three parties, we went to get into our car, and I noticed that one of the girls from the last party was with us. She got in the car. I said to her, "Hey girl, where are you going?" "With you guys," she replied.

So the three of us went to several more parties, and Susie, that was her name, knew people at all the parties that we went to. When the evening was over, I took Susie home. We exchanged phone numbers. The next day at Capitol, I received several messages from a "nobody." It was Susie. We met several times, and we established a very strong bond. We talked and talked. In time, she got herself a boyfriend and a job. We stayed in touch.

I went on tour with the Beach Boys, who insisted that I go to Michigan State University with them to shoot a concert they were doing. They called Capitol and told the president of Capitol that I would be on tour with them. When a moneymaking group, such as the Beach Boys, tells their recording company that they want a particular photographer to go on tour with them, the record company usually okays the request, as long as the record company gets the negatives. The day before the concert, we spent some time getting the feel for the place. That night at the concert, the campus rocked. The next day, as they prepared to go to their next gig in Paris, France, Dennis insisted that I go with them.

I explained that I didn't have any money or a passport, but Dennis said that everything would be taken care of. As the Beach Boys were going through two hundred pieces of luggage, looking for their passports, I sneaked away and got on a plane for Columbus, Ohio, to visit Susie and her parents. She had finally come home. She showed me all over town. It was October, and the leaves were changing into their beautiful fall colors. I went crazy shooting the leaves. After I returned to Hollywood, I received the most welcome letter from Susie's mom thanking me for giving back her daughter, alive. Susie had been on drugs and had attempted suicide several times. She had scars on her wrists to prove it. Years passed. We kept in touch, and now she's a happy wife and mother. We correspond regularly.

Back to the Beach Boys. Three of them were brothers: Dennis, Brian, and Carl Wilson. Mike Love was a cousin, and Al Jardine was a schoolboy chum. They were voted number one in the world by the United Kingdom music press, beating out the Beatles. "Good Vibrations" was the Beach Boys' greatest hit by this time. Things were getting hairy with all of their achievements. Dennis developed a serious cocaine habit and got involved with Charles Manson. Later, he drowned. After suffering severe nervous breakdowns as a result of drugs, Brian was sued by the remaining members of the Beach Boys for eighty million dollars. Carl became addicted to cocaine and alcohol.

My relationship with Susie was platonic. I could have done irreparable damage to her if I let it go the other way. I needed her, and she needed me. It was that simple. We went to different places together: Palm Springs, inner Los Angeles, novelty shows. We played volleyball and swam together, but most of all, we talked and talked and talked.

Timi Yuro was a classic. At age eighteen, she recorded "Hurt", her greatest musical achievement. I arrived at her home off The Strip and was greeted by her Italian mother who immediately offered me some of her very delicious spaghetti and meatballs. We shot inside and outside the house. I remember one particular shot that I liked above all the others. Outside, near her house, the sun cast a shadow from the top of the house. I made Timi stand right in the middle of it and shot half of her in the sun and half in the shade.

I drove Merle Haggard around for hours, looking for a suitable country theme for the next album that he was doing for. We went to the stables in Glendale and the railroad tracks that wound from downtown LA to Glendale. I had him run along the railroad tracks slowly and shot that, and then we went to a ranch in Santa Clarita, where I had him pose along a barbed wire fence with horses in the background. As I drove along, I would glance over to see him catching forty winks. He wrote such hits as "Okie from Muskogee." He was born in a boxcar, and much later, when he tried to support his family, he resorted to armed robbery and was caught and sent to San Quentin. While in prison, he joined the prison band; and when Ronald Reagan became governor, he gave Merle a full pardon.

A rock group heard about me and called to have their publicity photos taken. There were twelve of them, so I had to do some thinking to find the right locations. They were naive about Hollywood, so I took them under my wing and clued them in on what to expect from agents and promoters. I shot their photos, and while we were still going through the proofs, I got word that one of them had died from an overdose of drugs. So I took them out again and re-shot a lot of their photos with the new man. Shortly afterward, I heard that another member passed away from an overdose. They considered that a bad omen and decided to disband and call it a day. Good thinking.

As a favor from one rock group to me, I was offered a woman or a man for sexual purposes or a drug of my choice. I've always said no to these offers.

Working for Capitol had definite advantages. First, your name got around to the other recording companies. They would hire me for photo jobs. Henry Fonda was to appear as a guest on *The Merv Griffith Show*, which was a union house. That meant that a union photographer was to be at my side at all times while I did all of the shooting. He was to just stand there. They paid me, but they also had to pay the union photographer just for standing there and doing nothing. Most workers on a sound set in Hollywood were under the union: carpenters, electricians, painters, and yes, even photographers.

LOU RAWLS

I enjoyed shooting photos for an actor's portfolio. Usually his or her portfolio would consist of some straight headshots, something in an athletic outfit, some expressions, as a student, playing baseball, on a horse, on a motorcycle or roller skates, and anything else the photographer thinks an agent or casting director might like to see. The subject of what to do next usually comes up if the person is brand-new at acting. I've gone through it. I spend a little time explaining the ins and outs of the business, what a new person should do and not do, and where to get a free list of legitimate agents.

Every once in a while, I would get a letter from someone who saw my name listed in the credits on an album cover. I corresponded with two gals who lived on a farm in a remote area of Idaho. They were interested in Boyce and Hart, the duo who wrote most of the great Monkees originals.

In between photo sessions and when everything was caught up in the photo lab at Capitol, we would sit around in the front office and talk about nothing in particular. Our boss gave us an idea of what to expect in the coming weeks. He said that there was a British group coming to the States with the name of a bug. It was the Beatles. We were kept busy with them for quite a while.

My first contact with the Beatles came when they loaned themselves out to be photographed with kids in Beverly Hills for a fee of twenty-five dollars. It was a photo session for charity. The money was turned over to the City of Hope. The Beatles were very good to give concerts to raise funds for charitable causes. My boss and I took the photos as fast as we could load our cameras. Most of the Beatles's publicity photos and album covers came out of England. They were under contract to EMI, an English company and parent company to Capitol. There were times when the board members of EMI came to the USA on business. They all had British titles. There was Lord so-and-so and Sir so-and-so. It was a pleasure having them in the country.

My next contact with the Beatles came when they were ushered into the large recording studio at Capitol by way of a disguised laundry truck. We had the area secured, but Beatles fans were determined, and when they heard about the Beatles coming to Capitol, they arrived in droves. I placed myself high over the door on a slight platform where I remained the rest of the evening with my camera and a lot of film. No one got any unusual photos that night. We all shot from the same vantage point, so we all got the same photos. And when it was all over, everyone had the same shot as the next photographer.

For more than six months, there was an ad running in the papers about a man who was interviewing photographers for Liberty Records in Hollywood. I got my photos together and made an appointment. He looked at my stuff and pushed it toward me and said, "What makes you think you're a photographer?" My blood boiled. I gathered my wits and said to him, "What makes you think you're a human being?" I packed my photos and left. Once I got in my car, I realized that this guy probably spent all day, every day, interviewing photographers so that he could insult them and build up his own ego. I spoke to other photographers later who had gone in to see him, and he had done the same thing to them. And these were Hollywood's best. He had ads running for over a year in the trades, and he wasn't even an art director. The way I had it figured, he must have been related to some boss or other; otherwise, how could he possibly be in a position to hire photographers.

In the latter part of 1975, I was asked to shoot the upcoming Rose Parade in Pasadena on January 1, 1976. I was told where and when to pick up my pass, and the rest was up to me. I was to situate myself in a tower overlooking the corners of Colorado and Orange Grove boulevards. I had plenty of elbow room. The only other people in the crow's nest, as I'll call it, were the cameraman and male and female announcers. There was plenty of room for myself and the TV cameraman. We could both get shots of the corner of Orange Grove and Colorado as the floats rounded the corner. Hank Aaron was the Grand Marshall that year. I got some great shots of him being driven in a limo by one of the parade officials, and I was given a ribbon to pin on my shirt, which announced that I was part of the official parade. It got me into the float area and any other area that I wished to enter.

Herbie Hancock was a well known jazz artist. For his album cover, we shot at Shelly's Manne Hole on Cahuenga, and from there, we went to the beach. At Shelly's, I got a head shot, which was what we used for the cover. At the beach, we rested under a pier and talked. We were both from Chicago, so we did have something in common. We spoke of many of the places where I used to hang out and he was familiar with. Shearing, Miles Davis, Chris Anderson, and *Watermelon Man* were highlights of our conversation.

KHJ Radio hired me to be the photographer on the "Last Train to Clarksville," a promotion for the Monkees, the singing group. We boarded a decorated five-car train at Union Station and partied all the way to Del Mar, which is about a hundred miles south of Los Angeles. The train pulled into Del Mar, and somebody in a monkey suit crawled around the overhead entrance to the station where the sign read, "Last Train to Clarkesville." There were news photographers everywhere. Every car in the train had something going on in it. When we pulled back into Union Station that night, I had more than covered my assignment, and I had shot loads of publicity photos, which I turned over to KHJ. The promotion went well.

Jim Dunn, stunt man and professional deadbeat, hired me to shoot publicity photos of him. We shot for days, and I wound up with some great photos. We finally were to meet in a restaurant where I was to turn over the photos and get paid. He looked at the bill and said, "I'm not going to pay you one penny." He put the photos in his attaché and got up and walked to his car. I followed him to get his license plate, but he had it removed. Unfortunately, that was the only time I mentioned money. I was so interested in taking good pictures that I lost track of the money end of it. I found out that he was involved in porno, so I had the marshal serve papers on him to appear in small claims court. Of course, he never showed up. I still have the court papers and all of the negatives from that disaster.

Billy May was conducting a fifty-piece orchestra in the large recording studio at Capitol. It impressed me when Billy stopped all of the musicians in the middle of the recording to call attention to the fact that one musician out of the fifty hit a sour note. One out of fifty. Billy had written arrangements for Les Brown, Alvino Rey, Frank Sinatra, Peggy Lee, as well as Nat "King" Cole, and also wrote the theme for *The Man with the Golden Arm.*

I was invited to an apartment in Glendale to show my wedding photos and to see if they wanted to hire me to shoot their niece's wedding. They left me a good-sized deposit before I left. When I got home, I went to enter the wedding in my appointment book and discovered that I had double-booked for that day and hour. I called them back and told them the predicament I was in, but they wanted me. I offered to give them their deposit back. No dice. *This has never happened before,* I thought. I began calling all over town for another photographer to get these people off my back. I found one who was free that day and told him the story and paid him from the deposit that the client had paid me. He shot the wedding and evidently did a good job. I wasn't fearful of the aunt, but the groom was a muscle-bound big mouth who had threatened me. I was leery of the job in the first place, and I should have acted on gut feeling rather than financial gain.

I went to Chicago from Los Angeles on a visit and was asked by a Los Angeles client to personally deliver an envelope to an agency in downtown Chicago. While I was talking to someone at the Chicago agency, a very excited employee came into the room and whispered something in the ear of the person I was talking to. After a while, it was common knowledge that Brewster, the cat who had appeared in many TV commercials, had passed away. A savvy executive came up with the obvious answer—get another cat that looked like Brewster. Situation solved. How this obvious conclusion escaped the many people is beyond me.

I took out my list of locations to find a place to shoot a cover of the Classics IV, doing their hit "Traces." We started in Griffith Park. Nothing. Then James

Cobb said a friend of his owned a vintage automobile. I shot the group around the car. Still nothing. On a lunch break, we wound up at the park across the street from the Beverly Hills Hotel. Dennis Yost noticed an archway of flowers. I had a good feeling about this, so I shot the group arranged below the archway. I liked it, the Classics IV liked it, and the art director liked it, so we went with it. After all of that, the art director had most of the flowers airbrushed out of the picture. I kept in touch with some members of the group, but in time, we lost track of one another.

Wayne Newton was a pudgy seventeen-year-old kid who used to come up to Capitol with his brother, Jerry, who accompanied him musically. When Wayne returned after three months, it was obvious that he had lost a lot of weight and had managed to keep it off. He said that he was on a diet of grapefruit and soft-boiled eggs. I've never seen an audience as enthusiastic about an entertainer as Wayne's audience. His identifiable song, "Danke Schoen," became a Wayne Newton trademark, which he had performed thousands of times to eager audiences.

A producer at Capitol wanted to do an album on the sounds of race cars. George and I were assigned to take the photos, and engineers from Capitol were assigned to record the sounds. Some of us, including George, packed up our cameras and headed for the Winternationals at Pomona, California. We spent three days listening to and shooting the sounds of race cars. At night, while lying in bed, I could still hear the race cars in my mind. No one gave us earplugs.

The PR people at KHJ Radio were always thinking up new promotions. The Big Kahuna was one of their better ones. KHJ had a big listening audience, and they wanted to keep it that way. Someone at one of their Tuesday morning meetings dreamed up the Big Kahuna. So they hired Chris to dress up in a grass skirt and a headdress and gave him a spear, put some makeup on him, and voila, a south sea islander. I was to shoot pictures of him as he traveled through the city. He was to appear at a small airport after flying in on a helicopter. The crowd was huge, and the excitement was contagious. Kahuna signed bananas with a big X and gave them back to his followers. To top that, Kahuna went to Dodger Stadium with Ron Jacobs, a soundman, and me. He had hundreds of followers, so all you had to do was find the big crowd and follow it. The stopper for the day was when Kahuna stood up and pointed to the field of baseball players and said, "What that?" Ron Jacobs thought quickly and replied, "Tribal differences." To which, Kahuna replied, "Uh."

I was in Hollywood doing an assignment at one of the studios, when one of the girls came to me and asked me to shoot the weird billboards on The Strip. I got excited and spent the next three nights on The Strip shooting billboards.

JOHN
LENNON
ROCK'N'ROLL

When I finished, I took the photos to the girl who hired me and asked her, "Who do I bill?" She replied, "What do you mean bill?" Right then I knew that I had been taken in again. I thought I should develop a better sense of business. I showed my pictures of the billboard to some of my clients and managed to sell most of them. So it wasn't a total loss. I did get some of my money back.

Art Kevin, one of the newsmen at KHJ Radio, hired me to fly with him over a woody area of mid-California. He got a tip from someone that Patty Hearst was hiding out in a woody area. We saw nothing that looked suspicious, so we headed home.

An attorney running for political office asked me to shoot photos of him with the congresswoman from the San Fernando Valley, Bobbi Fiedler. We got to her office and were let in by the security person. Most congressmen or women have people on their payroll who tote guns and are responsible for their safety.

The Austrian consul general had a dinner party for Arnold Schwarzenegger and his lovely wife. He asked me to shoot photos of the three of them, which would appear in an Austrian magazine. By the time, my American bill was converted into Austrian money. I would get only a small portion of what I had asked for. Rather than embarrass the consul, I let the matter go.

Several times, I was hired to photograph recipients of an award given to citizens by the mayor of Los Angeles for outstanding achievements in the community. It could have been for an act of heroism or for giving back to the community or some other reason why the recipient received the award.

I kept my camera hung around my neck when I went down to skid row in Los Angeles. I wanted the men to see it and to be aware that I might shoot pictures at any time. When I was asked not to shoot pictures, I did not do so. Once I took my camera off my neck and put it behind some wooden boards. It wasn't long before one of the men snooped around and found it. I took it from him and went to my car and put it away. Every once in a while, I would take it out and shoot with it. I never felt completely safe. What would happen if one of them got hold of it and refused to give it back? I could get stabbed in the back.

Every week, KHJ Radio came out with a list of the top musical hits. There were always games and giveaways and searches all over town for specific items with hints given by KHJ disc jockeys while on the air. This kept the kids glued to the radio. What was in the huge boarded-up box on the lot in front of the KHJ studio on Melrose Avenue? And the winners either got what was in the box or another great gift. Mama Cass gave away a puppy to the winner of one contest, and there were those who won money or tickets to a concert. I was kept on my toes, but I got a lot of help from DJs like the Real Don Steele or Sam Riddle to be original in my photography.

Glen Campbell

Glen Campbell was the entertainer of a function at the Marriott on Century Boulevard. It was rather coincidental that right after I got the call to shoot Glen Campbell, I got a call to do a voice-over on Hawaii 5-0. They were both scheduled for the same day, two hours apart. I did the voice-over and raced to the Marriott on Century Boulevard and was able to shoot Glen Campbell. It took me virtually longer to sign the contracts on Hawaii 5-0 than it did to do my voice-over. Glen replaced Brian Wilson of the Beach Boys for a short time, but he was in demand for studio work at Capitol. He soon became an artist in his own right, making such great hits as "Gentle on My Mind," "Wichita Lineman," "Galveston," and "By the Time I Get to Phoenix."

I heard that Bobby Darin was difficult. I didn't find him that way at all. I was scheduled to go with him and an entourage of studio people to supermarkets, malls, parks, and various other places around the Southern California area over a period of two or three days. Bobby treated me with respect and dignity, and he was very gracious to his fans. He had contracted rheumatic fever at age eight and suffered because of it for years. Over the years, he became a singer, an actor, a dancer, and a songwriter.

Ty Hardin had a TV series in the sixties. I believe it was called "Bronco Lane." I got to know Ty from the Hollywood Christian Group. He married Marlene Schmidt, Miss Universe from Germany. In time, they had a baby girl. I spent many times with them in their Hollywood home, especially one very memorable Christmas *with* John Edwin and a few other guests. One Saturday morning, Marlene asked Ty to do the laundry. Ty's idea of doing laundry was to put everything in the machine all at once regardless of color. He thought it was a joke. Marlene did not. She tried to cover up her anger, but it showed through. When she went back to Germany, we corresponded for a while because that's the kind of person she was. I got the idea that Ty was very generous and free spirited.

At first, I thought Lawrence Welk was a boring old man who played a lot of bubbly music for the seniors. I hung out on the sound stage at ABC on Talmadge and Prospect and took photos of Mr. Welk mingling with the ladies in the audience. It turned out to be a happy time, with Mr. Welk dancing with as many ladies as he could. Some of the ladies would have adopted him if they could have. He was that popular. I've never seen a group of ladies as enthusiastic about an artist as these ladies were about Mr. Welk, except maybe Wayne Newton.

Miss Universe   Ty Hardin

Rock Hudson lived off of Coldwater Canyon up in the Hollywood Hills. I knew Chuck, one of Rock Hudson's friends, who did odd jobs for Rock. Chuck was a would-be actor, and now it was time for him to get some new publicity photos. Chuck thought it would be great if we did some photography using Rock's mansion as a background. But first, he wanted to show me around the grounds. He took me to the intimate small theater that was separate from the house. Chuck had done some work on it and was proud of his part. You could sit comfortably on pillows on the floor and enjoy a movie. As we were about to leave the kitchen, Rock came home, and Chuck introduced me. The two of them discussed business for a few minutes before Chuck and I went outside to begin our photo session.

Mark Spitz, swimmer and Olympic gold medallist, endorsed a game that looked very much like indoor tennis. A net was set up in the middle of the room, and the object of the game was to hit the birdie over the net to your opponent, and he or she has to hit it back and forth. My photos were to appear on the box that the game came in, showing Mark with paddle in hand swinging at the birdie. It was a dull shooting.

Bevel and Company advertised for people to join them in becoming members of a company that specialized in crazy games. One was a credit card that had written across its face "This Card Is Absolutely Worthless." Another one was a game like golf played with crooked shafts. The winner won other crazy items. There was never a shortage of people who sent in their money for membership and received their membership cards and a list of crazy games. I'll never forget the company because of two memorable things that occurred. The PR man for the firm had lunch with me one day uninvited. When it came time for the bills to come and pay for our meals, he shoved his bill over to me. I paid reluctantly but tested him the next time we had lunch by telling the waitress loud enough for him to hear that we wanted individual checks. He said, "Aren't you going to pay for me?" I said, "Absolutely not," paid my bill, and left. That was the last time he ate with me. The other incident was when I heard that Mr. Bevel got arrested. He hired young clean-looking college students to go to banks and transact business for him. Only the business was monkey business. His young employees were to hand the teller a sealed envelope, which, when opened, contained a note that stated, "This is a stickup. Put your money in this bag and don't sound an alarm." The young men were completely innocent of the entire escapade but walked out of the bank slowly with the bag of money and turned it over to Mr. Bevel. Mr. Bevel went to prison, and the college students were freed by the court.

A unique photo assignment was when I shot a newly appointed federal judge in her chambers dressed in her black robe with the American flag in the photo. She couldn't have been prouder. She explained her ideas to me, but she gave me license to do whatever I thought might make a good photo. It was a dark and dreary day in Los Angeles, but that didn't bridle her enthusiasm. She looked at her robe as a symbol of sovereignty and the American flag as a symbol of freedom and hope.

PART SIX

MINING

Cousin Mike met an elderly woman with mining interests near Lovelock, Nevada. She agreed to let Mike in on it if he could do some exploration. The ore of interest was antimony, a not too rare element used in chemistry, metals, and alloys. At one time, it was in demand, and Cousin Mike wanted me to explore the possibilities of mining and selling it. So I headed for Lovelock.

I met with Ed, a geologist, and Hap, an old-timer who had mined for the ore in the past. They were to share their expertise with me. I knew nothing about mining. There were two drawbacks: Ed had a very sick wife in a hospital in Reno, and Hap was missing his wife terribly. I waited in a motel in Lovelock for one of them to get back to me. Hap suggested that I take a thirty-mile drive out to the mine and climb some mountains and look for markers that were the boundaries for the mine. I had no idea why I was doing this. I found several tobacco cans nailed to trees with directions written on crumbly pieces of paper. This was the way the miners let others know that their mines have been recorded in the county office. I attempted to understand the whole process.

Both Hap and Ed were preoccupied with their wives. I wouldn't have had it any other way. I anxiously waited for one of them to give me directions other than looking for markers, but I did as I was told and, to avoid boredom, began following the railroad tracks to nowhere. This way, I couldn't get lost.

Close to the Fencemaker Mine, I bumped into a very determined young man sporting a gun on his hip. I greeted him, but he didn't respond. I was beginning to be concerned. We were thirty miles from town, down a dusty dirt road. What would happen to me if one of these miners were to turn on me in this unforgiving country with their guns and desert savvy!

I was slowly learning but still stumbling in the dark. Every chance I had, I wanted to learn more about the business of mining, but Hap and Ed were concerned about their wives and weren't able to spend as much time with me as I wanted.

Before I came to Lovelock, Hap had contacted a mining company interested in the antimony. Hap had sold about fifty thousand dollars worth of antimony and was on his second sale. But he also told me that he had seen the last of his mining days. As a parting gesture, he took me to his gold mine that had very little work done on it. We put just enough dynamite in it to improve the mine a hundred dollars worth, which is the minimal amount that you must invest in a mine annually to keep it in your name. The mine was just off of the main highway and didn't look like anything more than a huge hole in the side of a mountain. For five hours, I don't believe that one vehicle passed by on the road. Hap took dynamite sticks and showed me how to band them together and found a safe place to hide as they exploded and rocks flew through the air in all directions. Hap did a cursory examination of the fallen rocks and determined that there were no visible signs of gold. He really didn't expect to find any.

I get everyone's attention when I mention mining. Only a few people that I've heard about have struck it rich, and they are a rarity. The little money that Hap made on antimony went to pay for help, hire trucks for hauling it, for dynamite, for housing, and many other incidentals that new miners never consider when they strike out to get rich. You have to hit it really big to come out ahead.

Recently, I found notes that I wrote every day in a journal while in Lovelock.

Thursday

Left Los Angeles for Lovelock. Trip uneventful except for sheep and their herders on the road. Arrived 7:00 p.m. in Lovelock and checked into motel.

Friday

Ed (geologist) relayed a message that he would call me in the afternoon.

Saturday

I watched movie in the afternoon, *The Thomas Crown Affair*. There was only one movie shown once a week. You miss that one and you had to wait a full week for another one. After movie, dinner at Felix's. Ugh! There was nothing to brag about the meal.

Sunday

I was told to bring my gun from Los Angeles. I hiked up canyons and down valleys and began to feel good about my trip. Dinner at Felix's. In room, recalled Lawndale Bible Church in Chicago, I remembered hymns we sang and some of the people.

Monday

Hap had delivered one hundred and fifty tons of ore to a company that was buying it. He received half the money up front. Balance in two weeks. Went through magazines that I brought with me. Found pictures that I took

Tuesday

Actors' portfolios. I can't get away from them. Yuk! Terrible breakfast at Felix's. Cold toast, cold ham, and eggs. Coffee okay. Hap's truck not running so we didn't go out to the mine. I took my gun out to the desert with me. Put ice in my Styrofoam chest and took it with me just in case. Smart move.

Wednesday

Went to Fencemaker Mine with Ed and Jess Dullard. Looked for markers. Ed left and said he'd be in touch tomorrow. Poor Ed. His wife had cancer, and he's in Nevada with me on a mining venture. He says that once the markers are found, we still have to find the antimony.

Thursday

Ed and I went out to the Fencemaker over a long hot, deserted road looking for markers. I climbed every mountain in the area, but found only three. Ed said he thought the markers had been moved and later proved that they had been. Men with guns around mining claims . . . Ugh! While driving back to town tonight in the dark, for some strange reason, I think he was trying to scare me. He hit every major bump in the road at a high rate of speed. Yes, I think he just wanted me to go away.

Got the news that there were major fires burning in Bel Aire that so far had destroyed many homes. Can't get reception on radio in daytime, only at night. The cook at Felix's came out of the kitchen to my table and explained that he was not going to serve me the chicken that I had ordered because it would take too long. Of course I changed my thinking and ordered something easier for him to make, a sandwich. Every evening, the bus pulls up to Felix's and lets passengers off long enough for them to get a bite and gamble.

Friday

Heard a story about some miners hiring a prostitute to lure another miner away from his claim so they could claim it was theirs. Also saw remnants of a nearly deserted community near Lovelock loaded with rusty old farm equipment. It was practically deserted, except for a few would-be miners and a few old houses where they lived. They hung out in the local saloon and spent the day bragging to their buddies how they nearly made it big. It seems everyone has an interest in a mine because most of the talk around town is mine talk. Hap pointed out a house of prostitution a block from the main street.

Saturday

Asked Hap if I could bring him anything from Los Angeles. He said yes. Lobsters.

I called Cousin Mike, who said he would take care of it.

Friday

Left for Lovelock with six lobsters packed on ice. Don't know if Hap waited until he got home to share them with his wife. If I know Hap, he did. In time, the price of antimony went down, and we lost interest.

PART SEVEN

WEDDINGS

On a December 26, I got a call from an Internal Revenue Service (IRS) agent who said he wanted to get married before the New Year in order to take advantage of the tax break he would get for doing so. It took some doing on both our parts, but we pulled it off. I got to the church expecting just a few people. I was mistaken. The place was packed to standing room only. I don't know how the groom managed to get the tuxedos and gowns ready in time for the wedding, but he did. Everything went unusually smooth, and he got his tax deduction.

Every time I shoot a wedding and the bride and groom walk back down the aisle after being pronounced man and wife, I usually shoot a picture as they get to the back of the church. Funny thing but the bride has a smiling look of "I got him," while the groom has a perplexed look of "What happened?"

The mother of a bride came by to put a deposit for her daughter's wedding. She confided in me and told me that she was opposed to the wedding but that she was prayerfully going through with it for her daughter's sake. I shot the wedding, and then we all went to the hall where the reception was to be held. Everything was going fine until it was time for the cake cutting. The bride and groom posed for photos at the cake, and then it happened. The groom reached out to the bride and grabbed her by the back of the head with his left hand and, with his right hand, reached into the whole of the wedding cake and rubbed it in her face. She fought back as they chased each other around the tight space they were in. They were not smiling. I was unable to get photos without ruining my camera equipment. Later, when I delivered the photos of the wedding, the mother told me that her daughter had seriously thought things over and now wanted out of the union. The mother did pay me for the wedding photos and told me that it was worth it, just to show her daughter what kind of uncouth character he really was. The entire room where the cake cutting was supposed to take place was completely covered with cake.

Another's wedding that I shot in Santa Clarita ended, and everyone wound up back to the home of the bride and groom. The bride was an avid fisherwoman, and her new husband had a pond built behind their new home and stocked it with perch and bass. The bride got her fishing equipment and walked to the far side of the pond and made some beautiful casts. She caught some perch and bass while still in her wedding dress but threw them back.

At wedding receptions, the emcee takes control at a certain point and announces when the cake cutting will start, when the first dance will take place, and when the bride will throw the bouquet. A particular emcee, once he got the mike, told jokes, did a tap dance, sang a few songs, and acted more like an entertainer than a hired host. My time was running out, so I went to the groom and explained the problem. He couldn't control the emcee either, so I tacked on a few more hours on my bill.

A humorous incident occurred when a newly married couple went to Mexico on their honeymoon. While they were in Tijuana, they went to the bullfights. She stood up for the toreador, and he stood up for the bull. They fought violently over this and realized that they were incompatible. When they returned to the States, they insisted that the preacher give them back their wedding license. Of course, he couldn't do this. He had already sent it in. I've often wondered what happened to their beautiful wedding.

A sad event happened to a couple whose wedding I shot. After six months of being married, they went to Mexico on a vacation. The lady was killed in an auto accident. That was sad enough, but when her husband tried to bring her body back to the States for burial, the Mexican government said he would have to come up with fifteen thousand dollars. He was crying when he called me on the phone. He wanted the negatives of his wedding pictures. I saw to it that he got them. Very few times have I been to Mexico without paying some kind of bribe money to someone.

Our chef at the British consulate planned on getting married to his girlfriend. I offered free services as a photographer. We took two cars and drove to a wedding chapel on Wilshire Boulevard. The service was short. After the service, all five of us went back to the house for a brief celebration. We had cake and champagne. There was the consul, his wife, the bride and groom, and I. When the term of Mr. Finlayson, the British consul general, was up, he moved to the south of France where he had a home. He was kind enough to leave his address with me in case I ever went to France.

PART EIGHT

BOISE

I was in the air force being transferred to Gowen Field near Boise, Idaho, in the dead of winter. The temperature inside the railroad car that we were in was at least five below zero. It was unheated, there were no lights, it was about three o'clock in the morning, and the ride was a very bumpy one. Occasionally, we would stop for something or other. We would start up again, and the misery would start all over. *Why am I being treated this way?* I thought. I'm sure the air force paid a handsome price for that railroad car. Some railroad employee was taking advantage of the air force and put us in a worse than cattle car that could not be heated or lit. And to think that I was putting my life on the line by serving my country while that bastard sat on his fat duff behind a maple desk in a heated office. We sat in our respective seats with our winter coat collars pulled snugly up around our heads to keep ourselves as warm as we could.

When we got to Boise, a bus picked us up and took us to Gowen and let us out in front of a deserted barracks. The base had been deserted since World War II, and now there was nothing there except sagebrush and jackrabbits.

We worked a door open and went inside. Someone had a flashlight. I saw a potbelly stove in the corner. Some of us went outside and gathered sagebrush and stuffed the stove with it and lit it. The room soon heated to a point where it was tolerable. We made pillows out of our duffle bags and curled up on the floor. At first light, an NCO came around and invited us to a hot breakfast before giving us bags and ordering us to clean up as much sagebrush as we could and to fire up all the potbelly stoves that we ran across.

As more and more airmen poured into the base, there were more hands to help with the cleaning. In no time at all, the base took on a new face.

Some of us were reassigned to Mountain Home Air Force Base, which was just a short way from Gowen. It was quite a bit larger than Gowen. It too needed a lot of cleaning. Mountain Home was way out in the middle of nowhere.

There were no great memorable events that took place at Mountain Home except to say that during my stay in and around Boise, I met the most hospitable people you could ever meet. In fact, they were so nice that when I got discharged, I went back to Boise to live like so many other ex service men. I liked the people, their friendliness, their eagerness to help, and their thoughtfulness.

After discharge, I went to work for Ballou Latimer in Boise, an all-service drugstore with a photo department. I fit in well because of my interest in photography. At night, I worked at the Buffalo Club as a waiter, which is where I met Tom Kelly, another waiter.

We hit it off right away. Tom took me home to meet his mom and step dad. His mom told him to watch over me in case we had a Halloween night, which meant if a drunken cowboy came in and had too many beers and wanted to fight, he was to watch over me and not let anything happen to me. This was right up Tom's alley because he loved a good fight. My most memorable Halloween night was when someone said the wrong thing to Tom. He took off his apron and jumped over the bar and started swinging at this guy. They broke a coffee table and some other minor pieces of furniture. It wasn't long before they were out on the street exchanging fists. Just when I thought the battle was over and Tom's opponent wanted to shake hands, Tom hit him in the face, and the fight started all over again. When the fight ended, Tom thought it best if he went home for the night, which is what he did.

Sunday was a very quiet day in Boise. A few bartenders and waitresses would get together and take food and drink out to the desert and visit an old Englishman who had established himself in a ghost town. He was glad to have company. He ran a small grocery store where he kept a limited supply of canned goods and week-old produce that he sold to the lumbermen who drove lumber trucks to the lumber mill. Weekly runs were made to town to supply his store with a little bit of this and a little bit of that. Just enough to put some added groceries on the shelf and make his store look like a store. If he wasn't around and you wanted something from the store, you took what you wanted and left cash on the counter.

A stream ran through the center of town, dividing it. Most of the buildings were boarded up. Wooden sidewalks ran the length of Main Street. There were slats missing, so you had to watch where you walked. There were remnants of an old saloon, a blacksmith shop, a general store, and, on the outskirts of town, a few houses for the families that had lived there. There must have been a brothel.

We built a fire at the end of the street and had hot dogs and hamburgers and beer. Then we went exploring or sat with the old-timer, and listened to his stories. Late at night, we packed up our gear and drove back to town.

On other Sundays, we were entertained by two old ladies who played music for the tourists in Idaho City, another ghost town. One played an out-of-tune saxophone, and the other played the drums. There was never a shortage of tourist dollars for these two old, old ladies. And if you had a camera you could have your picture taken with the ladies for a price.

Because of the proximity of Nevada, there were people who lived in Boise part of the year and worked in Nevada in a gambling house the rest of the year. There were several families living in Boise who turned out their wives as prostitutes in Nevada with the consent of both husband and wife. An eighteen-year-old married woman stopped me on the street in Boise and said proudly, "Howard, I'm a working girl now."

A man who was alleged to have stolen fifty thousand dollars was holed up in a friend's house. Our crowd all knew of it, and we visited the house after hours and ate and drank with the whole family. I was checked out by the Boise police. They contacted the Los Angeles Police Department and found out that I was not wanted. I found this out through the grapevine. We knew things that the general public knew nothing about. I was in the in crowd.

Snowballs was the sporting bar in town. If you were looking for action or a good meal, you came to Snowballs. There were always card games being played there right out in the open. Farmers and businessmen, but mostly addicted players, filled the room. I say addicted players. I sent money to a friend to invest and he gambled it away. I never heard from him again.

Rosie, the friendly waitress, worked at the counter. She must have cleaned up on tips. For seventy-five cents, she would serve you the most delicious meat meal you ever tasted, and everyone tipped her big. She was worth it.

Bobbi got off the bus in Boise to look for work. She left her husband and two little girls back on the farm and came to Boise looking for a well-paying job. They were going through a rough time, and she thought she would try her luck in the big city. One night, she wandered into Grids Bar on Main Street while the exotic dancer was doing her dance. She said to herself, *I can do that.* She auditioned for the job and got it. She was good. She was very good. So now the farmer's wife turns into an exotic dancer. She called her husband and told him that she had a well-paying job. She sent money home, but she soon hooked up with a young stud in town and was beginning to like him too much. We were all hoping that her husband would come to town and take her back to the farm. No sooner had we wished it than it became a fact. Her husband came to town one day and announced that he too had found a well-paying job and that he wanted Bobbi to come back to the farm. Everyone liked Bobbi, but now it was time for her to head back to the farm.

A big transaction took place in the back room of a bar one day. One man had a large parcel of land with trees on it that he wanted to sell, and another man wanted to buy it. So they bought some beer and went to the storage room of the bar and negotiated for a couple of hours. When they came out, they asked a barmaid to witness the transaction. I believe the actual value of the land was a little over a million dollars. A tidy sum in those days.

If you ran up a bill in one of the businesses in town and needed a check to cover your purchase, the retailer or restaurant you owed the money to would ask you which bank you did business with. He would hand you one of two checks, and you take the one that had your bank on it, fill it out, hand it back, and you were on your way.

Flo was the greeter at the Buffalo Club and the best darn cooker of venison you'll ever meet, so she had the gang over many times to taste her savory concoctions. She knew many of the Basque sheepherders personally. Occasionally, I would see a Basque sheepherder walk down Main Street with a live lamb slung over his shoulder looking for Flo. The lamb would be bleating, and the sheepherder had the attention of everyone. Once the sheepherder found Flo and had given the sheep over to her, she would take it to a butcher and have it slaughtered; and once again, we would have another one of Flo's famous meals.

Les Wentworth and I used to meet to go fishing when we got off work at one or two o'clock in the morning. We were both bartenders, and now it was time to relax a little and enjoy our day off. Since Les was a native of Boise, he knew all of the best fishing spots. He would drive to a particular area, we would get some sleep, and at first light, we would begin fishing.

We came to a cliff that overlooked a winding river way down below us and lowered the raft by rope with our fishing gear inside. It was a challenge dropping ourselves over the side and slowly descending to where the raft was. We organized our gear, got in the raft, and went along with the current. Everything was going great as we caught our limit of fish, but when we wanted to go upstream, the current was against us. Les got out of the raft and went ashore and took the rope that was attached to the raft and pulled it upstream until he got us to where the car was high above us. We climbed the steep hill and towed the raft behind us. It became snagged on trees and boulders, but eventually, we got it to the top and put everything back in his car and headed out.

Les stopped to visit an uncle who lived in a log cabin with a friend. They were both sitting outside when we got there. They had no electricity or other modern conveniences, but they did have a lot of stuff lying around outside their cabin like automobile engines, fishing tackle, frames of old cars, pots and pans, small animal cages, hides from animals including buffalo and elk, and a lot of other things in their yard. The inside of their cabin was very dark. I could see why they spent most of their time outdoors. Their bed frame was made of heavy-duty logs, and the blankets were very thick buffalo hides. An old potbelly stove sat in the middle of the room with a stack of wood nearby. I'm not sure where they got their drinking or bathing water in the winter. Two old men living off the land.

I got to know one of the gals in town quite well. One Sunday, as I was about to leave and go back to the base, she asked me where I was going. I told her I was broke and was going back to the base. She opened her purse and reached in and took out a ten-dollar bill and gave it to me and said not to worry about paying her back.

A couple of days later, we were sitting in her front room, and there was a knock on the door. It didn't sound right, so I told her not to answer it. She insisted, went to the door, and opened it. A fist flew out and hit her in the mouth, knocking her front teeth out. She let out a bloodcurdling scream. I ran to see what was wrong. She stood at the front door of the house with blood dripping from her mouth, screaming. The person who hit her was a drunken airman from the base. Afterward, I tried to get her to prefer charges against him, but she wouldn't. She preferred to forget about the whole matter.

A very gorgeous girl used to come into Grid's Bar with her mother and two men. They would order their drinks and leave. There was never any problem, but I was told not to get friendly with them. The girl was supposed to have a six-inch-long hairpin in her hair and that she could be very dangerous if provoked.

My headaches were not getting better, so I visited the VA hospital in Boise and asked to see a doctor. I told him about the headaches and periods of depression. He listened and had the following advice: go home and write out a detailed autobiography. I did and brought it back to him. He looked at it rapidly and said that now that I brought my feelings to the surface, I would begin to feel better. I did not feel better but instead waited until I got to the Veterans Administration in Los Angeles and turned myself over to their mental health experts. Over a period of one and a half years, twice a week, I finally felt much better, with God's help. Some of the things I talked about with my therapists were: rejection, my mother, and women. In time, everything fit together.

After several weeks in Boise, a Basque bartender, threw me the keys to his room and told me to make myself at home. That was typical Boise hospitality. I spent the winter evenings in his room when it was too cold to hitchhike back to the base.

One of the secret illegal activities that went on in Boise were cockfights. I never heard of anyone getting caught at it, but I knew many people that bred their cocks to be the very best in the ring. Owners kept exact records on each of these cocks: the day they were hatched, their color, who they were out of, what they were fed, and what kind of care and training they got. I took a great interest in this sport as an interested outsider. I believe that every suburban town in the USA has some known illegal activity that the residents try to keep from the local law.

PART 9

SUSAN STRASBERG

Besides being a talented actress, Susan Strasberg was a nice person. I first met Susan while taking pictures of her and her daughter, Jennifer, on *The Dinah Shore Show*. Jennifer appeared on the show with her cardiologist, and Dinah Shore interviewed the two of them. Susan and I hit it off right away. She invited me to her home for dinners and get-togethers with other people in show business. She moved to a house on Densmore, in the Valley where she had a lot of land with fruit bearing trees and a lot of veggies growing. What we didn't have, we planted. After a good day of working in the garden, we would take a cool dip in the pool before having a laid-back barbeque dinner.

On holidays such as Thanksgiving, we would have the gang over for turkey or whatever Susan felt like making. At other times, she threw parties and invited people that she had worked with in the business: Cary Grant, Tina Louise, and Dyan Cannon, just to name a few. One Sunday, she invited all of us to come with her to Shelley Winters's Malibu home. When we got there, there was no place to park on the beach, so we turned around and came back home.

Lee Strasburg had a home in Hancock Park that had belonged to John Barrymore. On Sunday afternoons, he would have open houses for the famous and talented. He was known internationally as THE great drama coach and father of Susan. He would go into his library, put a record on and bathe in musical luxury, and leave his guests to themselves. He wasn't being rude. He was being Lee Strasburg. I took photos of Tina Louise's daughter at Lee's and gave Susan copies to give to Tina. I received a phone call from Tina thanking me and inviting me to a party, which, unfortunately, I was unable to attend.

I took Susan to see the motion picture *Rocky* at a screening. She became so obsessed with the picture that she stood up yelling enthusiastically when Rocky cracked open and swallowed the raw eggs. The movie audience knew that it was Susan.

Susan Strasberg and Jennifer

Susan told me about her best and worst movies. She mentioned one that I had never heard of before. When I asked her if it was playing anywhere around town, she said, "Don't you dare go see that movie. It was one of the worst things I've ever done." With some prodding, I got her to tell me about it. She played the part of a person with a growth on her back, and as it grew, her whole psyche would change. It didn't sound like anything I'd be interested in, so I assured her that I wouldn't go see it.

In time, I lost track of Susan but was informed by a cousin in Los Angeles that Susan had passed away. I have fond memories of the times we had. I also have fond memories of Lee's performance as the Jewish gangster in the motion picture *The Godfather*.

PART TEN

ACTING

I don't remember when I got my first acting job. I think it was as an extra in a militant movie about underground militiamen. I worked for one month under Taft-Hartley, and then I would have to join the union on the thirty-first day. That was okay by me because actors in Hollywood at that time would have given anything to be a member of the Screen Actors Guild (SAG) or the American Federation of Television and Radio Artists (AFTRA). Next, I did six months of afternoon soaps. In one week, I would do *General Hospital*; and the next week, *The Young Marrieds*; and somewhere in between, *Day in Court*. I kept very busy. These were all AFTRA. Then a friend who was the secretary to a casting director called me and said they needed someone who looked the part of a photographer for a major movie, *Valley of the Dolls*. She knew I was a photographer, so she suggested me. Besides, I could now join SAG, which I happily did. An added benefit was that I collected residuals (I got a check) every time the movie was shown. For twenty-five years, I got residuals for doing a small part in a major movie.

There were other movies that I did from which I collected residuals. One spoken word got you more than just a visual part in the movie. One sentence got you more than one word. A paragraph got you more than one sentence.

I was in a movie where I was seated in a church. We were to stand up and begin singing. I felt a sharp pain in my back. And again, I turned around and saw a fellow actor hide something behind his back. I hit him pretty hard. He fell and disrupted the whole scene that the director was directing. The director came over and asked what the problem was. I explained that this actor was jabbing me with a pin or a sharp object. The director took him out of the scene and told him to stand by. I don't know what happened to him. But when money is being spent on a production, the last thing you want to do is cause a delay in the shooting.

I had the pleasure of taking my cousin Mike's three kids on several of their many interviews for commercials and movie parts. When a number of kids would show up with their moms on a cattle call—that's what it's called—it can be a madhouse. You walk into this room and there are fifty kids, more or less, with their moms brushing their hairs and coaching them on what to say to the casting people and the producers. A selection was in the works, and now you go home and pray that you get a callback. If so, you go back, and there will be more questions, then you go home and stay close to the phone. There are many heartbreaks in Hollywood, but as I've told many of my photography clients, if they're really determined and keep going to interviews and try and try, they will get parts in movies or commercials. But they have to have stick-to-it-ness. Most kids who want to get into show business give up after a short while.

I once asked an assistant director why I was getting as many calls as I was. His reply was that he didn't have to go all over the studio looking for me. I was always close by. It was comforting to know that I was dependable.

Being a sometime actor taught me several things. Listen, concentrate, obey the director, be there on time, and if you leave the set, let the director know where you're going.

PART ELEVEN

SKID ROW

For seven years, I fed the men and women on skid row. I would start early on Sunday mornings with plenty of hot water and a lot of donated meat and vegetables. Within two hours, I would have the most delicious concoction. Stan Lim, the chef at my church, would donate the leftover prime rib bones with meat on them, or a hunter who had deer or elk in his or her freezer would gladly give me meat. I'd add a little bit of seasoning, throw in some vegetables, and voila, the soup is already. I was able to serve two to three hundred people, sometimes more. The regulars who were there every Sunday offered to help serving, which was an excellent idea. They knew skid row and could help assuage problems that were inevitable. Aside from soup and bakery items, we brought clothes and ice water and shoes; and once in a while, we would get our hands on some candy bars and bring them with us to distribute.

A young black man approached me one day on the street and said, "Hey, man, remember me? You fed me on skid row about a year ago." All of the years I spent on skid row, feeding the men, was suddenly worth it.

I made contact with a supermarket on Ventura Boulevard in the Valley. The manager told me to come over on Saturday, and he would load me up with all of the one-day-old breads, pies, cakes, and whatever else he had from the bakery. We would wait until we had passed out all of the soup, and then we would dump all of the bakery goods on the ground, and there would be a mad scramble for those items.

There was a lot of violence on skid row. We had the men line up for the soup, and one man insisted on being at the head of the line. He pulled the man at the head of the line out and pushed him to the ground. The man on the ground got up, reached into his pocket, and pulled out a push-button knife.

They fought for a couple of minutes and knocked all of our soup on the ground. Nobody got soup that day.

Some of the men removed the bricks from the side of a building that housed a toy distributor and entered the building through the hole in the wall. I'm still trying to figure out what skid row habitués were going to do with toys. Some other men were hired to patch up the wall with a plate of thick metal. They had the plate of metal all lined up, but there were metal bolts sticking out of the building on the outside.

An elderly Hispanic man staggered to the building and cut his head on one of the protruding bolts. He began bleeding profusely. I got in my car and drove to the nearest phone and dialed 911. The dispatcher said, "Oh, so the sidewalk popped up and hit you in the face huh?" I said, "No, you bastard. A man's bleeding to death, and you better get an ambulance here immediately." The ambulance wouldn't enter the parking lot until the police came. Everyone put on rubber gloves. The Hispanic man didn't understand English and fought off the paramedics. The paramedics prevailed and managed to get him bandaged, but once they left, he removed the bandages. At least the paramedics did their job.

We made friends with Hope, a well-educated Hispanic lady who had become a member of skid row. I liked Hope. She came to me one day and said, "Honey, you got two dollars? I need two dollars." I pulled her aside and said, "Hope, you won't lie to me, will you? What do you want with two dollars?" She started to cry. "I won't lie to you. I got to get drunk." I said no, and she walked away. Another day was a real Halloween. We sensed it when we drove our cars onto the parking lot. There were about fifty men arguing and cursing one another mostly in Spanish. I saw Hope in the middle of it and kept my eye on her. Hope yelled something at one of the men in Spanish and started to walk away. She got about twenty feet when she decided to come back at the man, all the while cursing him in Spanish. He picked up a two-by-four and, assuming the position of a baseball batter, drew the two-by-four back and swung it fully in her face. She fell to the ground bleeding and crying. The man that hit her went to her while she was lying on the ground and kicked her. She was a total mess, her dress covered with blood. I stayed out of the whole incident, fearful that I would get a knife in the back.

There are a lot of people with mental illness on skid row. One Vietnamese war veteran carried around a sixteen-square-inch board with nails driven into it to form letters. The nails spelled out that the whole problem in the world was due to the IRS. He would sit in the parking lot and hold up the board.

I didn't know Bill's story. He looked like a skid row habitué, but he was sane. He carried around his possessions on his back and slept under the freeway near a duct that spit out warm air all night. Sometimes late at night, he would work at the Central Market, which didn't open for business until midnight, when trucks would load up on produce and drive back to their respective supermarkets and stock the stores with produce for the day. It was a busy outlet. At about six o'clock in the morning, they would close the door and overheads and would go out for breakfast. But the trucks hauling the produce would now pull up to the back door of a supermarket, getting ready to unload their produce for the day.

I heard loud voices coming from a group of men on skid row. One of the men started running. Another man took off after him, caught him, and pushed him to the ground. They wrestled for a while before the second man took out a pair of handcuffs and put them on the man. It was a drug bust. The cop took out a walkie-talkie and called the police to come and pick up the perk. This was a common occurrence on skid row.

There was a shack about a block from where we set up on Sundays to give out the food with always a pot of coffee on the stove. Normally, it housed indigents who were lucky enough to discover it. There was a bitter feud between opposing gangs who each claimed it as theirs. No one had papers to prove who actually owned it. It was just there. One Sunday, as we arrived to feed the men, there were fire trucks on the scene, and there was now a pile of rubble where the shack had stood. Someone had torched the shack.

I took hundreds of pictures on skid row, but it got to be hairy. Several times, men on skid row tried to steal my camera. I learned to put my camera in my car and lock the door. I took pride in my photos, and today I have a series of outstanding photos about all that happened. One set of photos I have tells a story of a Sunday when I happened to get some prime rib bones with a lot of meat on them. The men chewed the meat off the bones and threw the bones into the garbage. A latecomer staggered to the garbage, got on his hands and knees, and reached into the garbage and pulled the bones out and chewed what little meat there was off of the bones.

There was a well-dressed black man leaning on a car in the parking lot. He waved over to me and asked me where I was from. I told him that I was from the south side of Chicago. He called me South Side. He asked me to bring him a cup of soup, telling me that he was a member of the Bloods, a black gang that was constantly at war with the Crips, an opposing black gang. Both gangs had done their share of killing each other. He confided in me and told me that he thought there were some Crips in the crowd, and because he was all alone, he probably couldn't put up much of a fight if he were attacked. I brought him a second cup of soup. That was the only time I saw him.

PART TWELVE

WAITING

I did my first waiting job for my friend Tedd. He called and said he needed help to work a director's reception at his home. I was to serve drinks and finger foods to the guests, set up at the beginning, and clean up at the end of the reception. I found it easy work and got very easy money. There were other people who were hired to do the same thing. We exchanged phone numbers, and pretty soon, I was getting calls to work other receptions as well as formal dinners.

At that one particular reception, I recognized many of the celebrities, James Garner and Penny Marshall and many others. I didn't ooh and aah over the celebrities.

Much of my work came from consul generals. In time, I worked for every major consul general in Los Angeles, including the British, the Austrian, the South African, the Australian, the Japanese, the Italian, the Turkish, the Canadian, the French, and their trade people. If I was seen at one consul's residence and another consul came as a guest, it wasn't unusual for the guest to get my name and number from the host and call me. I built up a reputation with most consuls and sometimes worked every night of the week alternating between one consul and another. At first, I worked for the caterer; but in time, the host would call me directly and hire me to make sure they got me and not someone who was hired by the caterer. If the caterer ordered me to do something, I politely reminded him or her that I was hired by the host. This created bad feelings of course.

I also worked for Gregory Peck, Bob Hope, and Walter Matthau. To me, they were just ordinary people. Of all of the celebrities that I worked for in Hollywood, Gregory Peck was the gentleman of all gentlemen.

I'd like to get a story straight that I overheard another waiter tell his clients. We had a new chef at the British consul general. When he shopped for the formal dinner, he bought only ten pieces of chicken for ten people. When serving time came, two guests took two pieces of chicken each, leaving two people without. The wife of the consul saw the predicament and leaned over to one of the guests who had two pieces and whispered, "You got to give one piece back." The guest with two pieces leaned over and scooped one piece onto the plate of the guest who had no chicken. I hurried into the kitchen and told the chef the problem and asked if he could make something quick for the consul. He said he couldn't, so I went back into the dining room to check on everything. I took the incident personally although it wasn't my fault. The consul general was the only person who didn't get his chicken. After the party was over and the guests left, the consul general, Mr. Finlayson, came into the kitchen laughing and commented about the look on my face when I stood in the middle of the floor holding an empty serving tray. I'm glad he saw humor in it.

In 1982, the Turkish consul general was assassinated by a young Armenian as his car stopped at a red light. Everything at the Turkish consul's residence changed. The Turkish government bought the house next door and posted Turkish and local police. They put cameras in the trees in order to immediately recognize cars that pulled up outside. When I would park on the street, I was aware that I was on camera. The iron-wrought gate would automatically open as I approached it, and as I walked to the house next door, I would glance over to see guns mounted on the walls, some big and some small. Two or three heavily-armed Turks would greet me. They were very friendly. The property next door to the Turkish Consulate before the assassination had belonged to Nat "King" Cole. I had been in it when Nat was alive and I worked at Capitol.

Once I found out what the menu was, I would set up the table if it were a formal dinner or set up a bar if it was an outdoor reception. I usually hired as many people as I thought we needed once I got a count of the guests.

Nur, the Turkish chef, was very talented and made the most delicious baklava, hummus, and all of the Middle Eastern foods that I like. Because they are Muslim, they didn't drink alcohol but did serve light alcoholic beverages to their guests. When I first received a call from them for my services, they asked me about my background. I knew what they were looking for. I told them my people came from Lebanon and Syria. I didn't hear from them for six months, but after that, they began calling me. I worked for them for fifteen years.

Anwar Sadat from Egypt was the luncheon guest at the home of Chancellor Young of the University of California at Los Angeles. When I arrived, I was told by the FBI where I could park, and I could not go back to my car once I was in the house. The FBI had German shepherds sniffing out the bushes. The four Egyptian security guards ate lunch in the same room as Mr. Sadat. I walked over to them and said, "The food is good, but nothing like our Arabic food." They didn't acknowledge me. When Mr. Sadat was ready to leave, his ten or so vehicles outside all started their engines at once. A young, attractive secret service agent pulled up her cuff and whispered in it, "They are ready to leave now." She was wired. The first vehicle in line outside was a motorcycle, then an ambulance, then Mr. Sadat's car, followed by the others. The entourage zigzagged down the hill to the street.

I always knew when the British consul was having royalty at a formal dinner or for a reception. I would ask Jennifer, the consul's secretary, who the guest of honor would be. If she said, "I can't tell you," then I knew it was royalty. Royalty would always sign the guest book with just their first name. Phillip would sign the book Phillip, whereas regular guests would put down their complete name and address. When Princess Anne was a guest, I was asked to follow her around with a can of Coca-Cola on a tray and serve it to her when she asked for it. When she dove into the pool, a Scotland Yard policeman dove in. When she got out, he got out. I enjoyed working at the British consulate for eight and a half years— first for Mr. Finlayson and then for Mr. Ballantine. Jennifer referred me to Mr. Ballantine. She said she liked the way I presented myself during formal dinners and receptions.

I was called to the British consul's residence on June Street and was told that there was to be a very important small informal meeting. When I arrived, I was stopped at the curb by two men in raincoats who had my name on a list. Inside were eight more men and an attractive young lady. I was instructed on what to do when the doorbell rang. I was not to answer the doorbell, but let one of the men answer it. I was to go into the room where the meeting was to be held every ten minutes and ask if anyone needed anything and bring it to them. In the kitchen were drinks and the makings of sandwiches: pickles, bread, lettuce, tomatoes, and sandwich meats. Some of the men had Irish accents. After a while, I deduced that the meeting had something to do with the Irish Republican Army. The consul, Mr. Ballantine, was not in the meeting, but I believe that he loaned out his home for the meeting. He loafed around all evening in his comfortable clothes. I counted a total of about eight men. I knew that they had guns. A young lady took part in the meeting. At the end of the evening, I was paid and went home.

I was hiring a lot of my people to work various parties, especially consular receptions and formal dinners. I tried to get as much information from the consuls as I could, so I would know who the guest of honor was, where he or she would be seated at the table, and if there was anything special I should know about serving them. I received calls from the secret service requesting a list of the help so they could do a check on them. The usual request was for the birth dates and social security numbers of all the people that I hired for that evening's affair. That was all they wanted. I got quite a few calls from the secret service.

I worked for Mr. Drake, the South African consul general. He and his wife lived in a high-rise in Santa Monica overlooking the Pacific Ocean. I was serving them one evening as the sun was setting. I commented on the beauty of it all. Mrs. Drake said that she would like to have me over for dinner some evening. We would eat on the terrace and watch the sun descend into the ocean. They did call me, and of course, I accepted and asked what I could bring—maybe a bottle of wine or something. They assured me that they had everything, including South African wine, which was the best. Mrs. Drake was a very talented cook. She made the hors d'oeuvres, the main course, and the dessert. What a treat! I went home completely satisfied with a bottle of delicious South African wine.

The Japanese consul had the secret service call me to give them information about the help. A young monarch was the guest of honor, and the secret service was inconspicuously all over the house. At dinner, the young monarch was to be served first and then the rest of the guests in order of age and rank. Nobody speaks until the guest of honor speaks. There was no small group having a conversation that didn't pertain to the guest of honor. All attention was to be on the guest of honor. The Japanese always have at least five or six courses, and sometimes more. When the guests retire to the living room and the table is cleared, the help gets to eat a delicious Japanese meal.

Every four years, the consul's term would be up, and we would get a new consul. I might work at one consul's residence for fifteen years but always for different consuls.

Mr. Hutton Wilkinson was one of my favorite party givers. As it goes, Mr. Wilkinson was looking for property in Hollywood, and a real estate agent showed this particular property to him. He later found out that his father had owned it. He bought it and decorated it beautifully. From the outside, it didn't look like much, but from the inside, it reeked of elegance. Splashy controlled colors in every room. Pillows and drapes and chairs and wallpaper and dinner settings were all elegantly done. The backyard had a personality all its own, including an elongated pool with statues at the far end spitting out water, surrounded by well-groomed greenery.

A colleague of Mr. Wilkinsons, Tony Duquette, lived high in the Hollywood Hills in a canyon not too far from Picfair. Both inside and outside of his house was decorated like a museum. One of the rooms had paintings that lined the walls from top to bottom with soft, indirect lighting. When Mr. Duquette hired me to serve dinners, it was always out on a narrow balcony overlooking statues and pagodas and narrow, indirectly lighted bridges and temples of oriental motif. His home was a museum both inside and out. I got permission from Mr. Duquette to photograph his house over a period of several days. We were on very good terms.

I became popular with the consul generals. I was older than most of them, and I did an excellent job. It got to the point where I would serve four or five consuls a week, sometimes more.

There were very few consuls, if any, whom I refused to work for. I should never have taken a job from the Belgian consulate. The children and their friends kept stealing bottles of liquor from the bar when I needed them most. When I discovered where the bottles went, I had to go into the kitchen and wrestle the bottles away from the kids who were of drinking age but who were very inconsiderate. One of the female children had her chair tilted back, her legs propped up on the table with her dress up to her thighs, drinking from the bottle. I grabbed the bottle out of her hand, but in a little while, she came back and got it again. When the evening was over and everyone left, I was paid and told to clean up and leave. Everyone had left. I went to get in my car and found a motorcycle lying on the ground right behind my car. I moved it but then found that the exit gate was locked. I had to take out tools and remove nuts and bolts from the iron gate, lay it on the ground, and drive over it to get out. I was extremely glad to get out of there and breathe fresh air again.

I felt very comfortable working for consul generals. I had a little saying that I always told the people that I hired to work with me: Always smile, and when addressing guests, always say, "Yes, ma'am," "No, ma'am," or "Yes, sir," "No, sir."

Mr. Myet, the French consul, was very cordial. He had seen me at another consulate, asked about me, and hired me to do his receptions and dinner parties. I would usually have everything set up so that when he arrived from the office, he could go to his room, freshen up, come out, and begin meeting the guests. I thought that we would be serving the best French cuisine, but there was nothing special about the food. It was very good, but it was typically American. I don't know just how much the consul wanted to have a say in what was being served.

Pierre hung around the French consulate, but for some reason, he was not hired to do anything. I did know that he wanted my job. On Bastille Day, we were to set up outside the campus of UCLA, on the grass. I had all the wine cooled, all of the glasses unpacked, and all the help I needed. Then I saw Pierre walking over to where we were setting up. He reached down under a table and began removing cases of wine. He took five cases and put them in his car. I questioned him. He said that the consul asked him to come and take the cases of wine. By the time I found the consul and asked him about this, Pierre was long gone. The consul said that he hadn't told Pierre to take any of the cases. I had witnesses just in case Pierre would tell the consul that I took the five cases of wine.

I did a lot of hiring for Bastille Day, Japanese National Day, British National Day, Turkish National Day, and other countries' national days. The respective consuls would go to the mike and speak for a short time, and then they would play their countries' national anthems, then the American national anthem. The flags of the two countries would be flown next to each other and there might be a presentation from the USA to the guest country by the mayor or the mayor's secretary. This was always very well done.

Mrs. Windsor, the Canadian consul general, was a super delight to work for. When she came downstairs and saw me, she would always comment that now she knew that the party was going to be a success. She belonged to the Molson family, so there was always a great amount of Molson beer in her garage. One memorable event was when a guest started talking and talking and talking and talking. He wasn't the guest of honor but just a regular guest. Nobody ate. It was embarrassing to one and all. I don't remember what happened, but I do remember that someone commented later that they wished he had been quiet and given the consul a chance to say something.

There was an outdoor reception for a dignitary at the Japanese consulate. The best Japanese hors d'oeuvres were served. I couldn't help but notice an American lady go through the shrimp line again and again until I finally saw what she was doing. Once she got her order of shrimps, she would walk about ten feet, glance over her shoulder to see who was watching, and tilt her shrimp plate into her purse. It was quite humorous.

I was flattered to learn that a customer made a notation in her will that after she passed away, she wanted me to work at her memorial service and to hire the help. She evidently had faith in me when I served her during her lifetime. When her daughter called me to make the arrangements, I thought it was a joke, but then I realized it was for real. I did my best in her honor.

Even more flattering was when a client called and asked me what days I was free. She was building her party around my schedule. You had better not let someone like that down.

Lest I make it sound like I was the only person that could make a client happy, no way. There were many instances that I recall where I lost a few clients. A lady that I could count on for parties and dinners asked me to get help for an upcoming party. The minute my help arrived, the host and my hired help hit it off. I was never called again. Or the time a big Hollywood producer had me bring help. Once the wife of the producer met my friend, I was never called again. She commented on how helpful he was. Not that I was not helpful, it's just that they hit it off. Or the time the Swiss consul had me bring extra help. Their Filipino house girl was friendly with the Filipino house girl at the Austrian consulate, who did not like me. So they told their employers, and their employers hired someone other than me. You win a few, and you lose a few.

Bob Hope's secretary called me to work one evening. I was told by Ingrid, the cook, that I would be serving just Mr. and Mrs. Hope. There were no other guests. The meal was ready. Mr. and Mrs. Hope came downstairs, I pulled the TV out from the wall, they made themselves comfortable, and I served them.

After half an hour, they got up and went to bed. They had always been easy to work for.

About eight years prior to this, their houseboy refused to pay for half an hour that I had worked on a holiday, which normally was double time. I called and questioned his reasoning. His answer was "Well, you ate, didn't you?" In all of thirty-five years of waiting, I have never been docked for eating. I called Mr. Hope's secretary and told her about the incident. She said she would take care of the matter, and she did.

The golf course behind Mr. Hope's house catered to the extremely wealthy. I looked at the roster one day and saw that nearly every name on it was a top name in show business. The managers of the course were very generous and, on more than one occasion, closed the course to let a charitable organization use the course to raise funds. I was on the course shooting photos for the City of Hope and saw Mr. Hope driving by in a golf cart. The next time I worked for Mr. Hope, I was in the kitchen and asked Ingrid, the cook, what Mr. Hope was doing out on the golf course when it had been handed over to the City of Hope for the day. She motioned for me to come closer and whispered, "Howard, Mr. Hope owns the golf course." Oh!

The first time I worked for Gregory Peck, I went down to the lower level of his house on Carolwood Drive and saw Johnny Carson, Gene Kelly, Liza Minelli, Jack Lemmon, Walter Matthau, Frank Sinatra, and forty more top celebrities. When the party ended, Mr. Peck went behind the bar to get something, and I asked him about one of the pictures on the wall from the movie *Gunfighter*. For the next hour or two, he fascinated us by telling us the background behind all of the photos on the wall.

Another man and I were hired to serve a formal dinner for the Pecks. The other waiter had Mr. Peck's table. I had the table with Frank Sinatra, Louis Jordan, Mrs. Peck, and five other guests. Mrs. Peck asked me to go to the kitchen and wet a towel and bring it to Mr. Sinatra. I did and returned to the table and handed it to Mr. Sinatra. He felt it and, very dissatisfied, said, "No, no, bring it to me with warm water and more wet." I went back to the kitchen and did as I was told and returned with a warmer, wetter towel and handed it to Mr. Sinatra. He stood up and put his face in mine and said, "You f—" I'm so glad everyone at my table heard him. I thought it best if I disappeared into the kitchen. I told the help who all agreed that if I went back immediately, he would have completely forgotten about it. Not that he was a forgiving kind of person, but he was losing it. Mrs. Peck must have told Mr. Peck about the incident because the next day, I received a phone call from Mr. Peck saying that he had heard about what happened at my table and that he wanted to apologize for the behavior of "that man." He didn't use the name Frank Sinatra because in Hollywood, the walls have ears, and you have to be careful not to use real names. I called Mr. Peck back and got his lovely wife. She said that Mr. Peck was resting and asked if she should awaken him. Of course not, I said. But I told her to relay my message to him. We spoke for about fifteen minutes about the incident, and she too used the term *that man*, but not once did she use his real name. I got along well with Mrs. Peck, but I told her never to put Frank Sinatra and me together again. We both agreed that this was a good idea. We wound up our conversation by both of us agreeing that Frank Sinatra was a great talent.

Before leaving for Colorado, Mr. Peck contacted me to work a swim party on the Fourth of July 1997. I informed his secretary that I was moving to Colorado and that I would be ever so grateful if Mr. Peck would write me a letter of introduction in case I sought the same kind of work in Colorado. I received a beautiful "To Whom It May Concern" letter recommending me highly. That's the kind of person Mr. Peck was.

I got an invitation from Mrs. Nancy Mehta, wife of Zubin Mehta, conductor of the Los Angeles Symphony Orchestra. Mr. Mehta's daughter was being officially indoctrinated into an Indian Religion. After the ceremony, they served a real Indian feast. The foods were foreign to me but super delicious. I learned something about Zubin Mehta that night. You could get him into a mellow mood by surrounding him with beautiful women. He laughed and told jokes to the help and was completely relaxed. All the help that I hired that night were well experienced and well seasoned. The best.

Steve Lawrence and Edie Gorme were guests at a party I worked on. They came into the kitchen to take their shoes off and relax. They were real down-to-earth people.

Once a month, I was hired to work a dinner party for the American Society of Cinematographers (ASC). I was allowed to hire as many people as I thought was needed. The guests were the world's most talented motion picture photographers. After dinner, they would be lectured on new motion picture optics or any innovations in the realm of motion picture cameras.

Writers have got to be interested in people and things to be effective. Louis L'Amour had that quality. I had the pleasure of serving Mr. L'Amour at his home off of Sunset Boulevard. I had a few moments to spare, so I wandered into Mr. L'Amour's library. He had numerous books on all four walls. And behind these moveable walls, he had more rows of books. I was looking through his library when Mr. L'Amour came into the room and announced himself. I told him I was interested in his vast library. He took a book from the shelf and told me a little about it. Then he asked me where I was from. I told him Chicago, and he began asking me questions about Chicago. Before I knew it, he was listening to every word that came out of my mouth. I was very flattered to have this world-renown author take an interest in my background and me. I had to get back to work but couldn't get over the fact that I suddenly was of interest to this great author. On the way home that night, I couldn't help but review in my mind the brief encounter I had had with this man of letters.

I'm not one to remember people's names, but I was very impressed with Anne, of British royalty, who was a guest at the home of the British consul general. She was to greet members of the foreign press. They lined up in the yard of the British consul general. There was to be at least thirty or forty of them. I thought how she could remember all of their names and their home countries. But without hesitating, she started at one end of the line, went from person to person, shook their hands, greeted each of them by name in their native tongue, and carried on a brief conversation. I was very impressed.

The German consul general had an afternoon cocktail reception. One of his guests asked for wine in a champagne glass. I served it to him, but when the consul general noticed the glass, he berated me in front of his guests for using the wrong glass. I told the consul that his guest had asked for his wine in a champagne glass. His guest backed me up. I got a dirty look from the consul. That was the last time he hired me to work for him. That was one type of personality I had to put up with. Most of the consuls treated me with respect, but there were exceptions.

PART THIRTEEN

MEXICO

I became acquainted with the Russell family through a gal that I worked with at Capitol Records in Hollywood. There were four brothers and a sister, Jane. I became pretty tight with two brothers, Tom and Jamie, and Jamie's wife, Pam. Tom had always wanted to fly, so he took flying lessons; and when he found out that many of the pilots he knew were flying to a place in Mexico named Punta Final, he soon joined them.

It wasn't long before Tom rented a piece of property on the beach in Punta Final. We now had our own little community. We towed a trailer down and established it on the beach next to a dozen other American trailers. After he got the trailer in place, he built a walkway around it to place a butane refrigerator. Now we had the luxury of keeping our meat frozen and our food refrigerated. I doubt if the cement walkway lasted because it was made with seawater, which has a high concentration of salt in it.

When flying to Puertacito in Mexico, you have to make your own runway between the heavy patches of sagebrush and tumbleweed. Rabbits and coyotes would scurry to get out of the way. Once the plane is on the ground, it becomes quite bumpy until we come to a complete stop.

If you drive to Punta Final from Los Angeles, you have to count on three to four days of travel time. There are huge boulders on the Mexican roads that must be removed, and several passes are too narrow for the trailer to get a trailer through without help. If you find yourself in that situation, wait for the next American to come by because if you can't pass, then neither can he. He must help you because if he doesn't, then nobody goes anywhere.

One night, while hauling a trailer loaded with supplies, we came to a very steep hill. Our truck couldn't make it up the hill, so we waited until morning and in daylight unloaded the truck and placed everything along the road. We then drove the truck up and then down the hill and carried everything back to the truck and reloaded it. The rest of the trip was a snap.

We needed airplane fuel one day, so we flew into Puertocito. There was a note on the locked door of the hangar saying that they were in town at the local pool hall. We walked to the pool hall and found the men from the airport. They insisted on playing a few more games. We all walked back to the plane hangar. One of the men took the lock off of a fifty-five-gallon drum and pumped out gas with a hand pump. We fueled the plane and took off for our place in Punta Final.

We were waiting for a couple to fly down from Los Angeles in a converted B-25, but it was getting darker by the minute. Suddenly, we heard the sound of an airplane overhead and could see their lights. We got some land vehicles and shone its lights on a makeshift landing strip. We had a fire going down at the other end. They made several passes but landed safely. We excitedly ran to them and formed a circle around them. No one saw the huge snake in the middle of the circle. When we did finally see it, we ran back to the trailer and spent the rest of the night talking and enjoying the peacefulness and serenity of the Mexican gulf.

I was asked by Tom Russell to deliver a refrigerator to a family that he had befriended in Tijuana. I put all of my money in my shoe, and a friend and I made it to the border late one night. The Mexican Border Patrol stopped us and asked what we had in the truck. I told him we were delivering the refrigerator to a poor family in Mexico. He held up his hands and said, "No, we build our own refrigerators here in Mexico." That was a big, fat lie. He motioned me to a little telephone size shack and asked me if I had any money. I turned my pocket inside out and gave him the six dollars that I had put in my pocket. "Are you sure you don't have any more money?" I threw up my hands. He waved me through. Mexican border agents are known for their acceptance of bribe money.

After delivering the refrigerator, we wandered around the interior of Mexico for a day. At night, we stayed in a rundown motel with no air conditioning. We were given a huge fan to put at the open door to pull the stifling heat out. It sat on the floor at the open door with all the windows open.

It's the people living in the border towns that you have to be leery of. The hustlers have learned that's where the money is, and they're out to get their share. The population in the interior of Mexico was very hospitable and helpful. They'll go out of their way for you.

In one village, it must have been movie night. People were literally hanging out of the windows from the second floor, and there were those who were waiting in line to get in. The heat must have been stifling.

PART FOURTEEN

COLORADO

In 1995, I left Los Angeles and headed to Chicago for a vacation, but first, I was to stop in Cedar Rapids, Iowa, where I was born, and meet up with cousins, Terry and Martha, at a convention made up of all the people who migrated from the village of Ain Arab in Lebanon to the United States. I got as far as Vail Pass in Colorado before my radiator blew. I got towed into Vail, and after four days, I had another one installed. The mechanic told me that I had engine problems and that I better not drive further without having the engine repaired. Since he didn't have the needed parts, he towed me to a garage in Gypsum, Colorado. While waiting for the repairs to be finished here, I got a room in Eagle, Colorado, and was told by the management that there was a fair and rodeo in town. I went to the fair and met Sarah Fisher, the Eagle County clerk. Since it was too late to go on to Chicago, I headed back to Los Angeles; but before leaving, Sarah invited me back to work at the rodeo the next year. I returned the next year and met the Lagace family: Kevin, Cindy, Addie, and Noel. After three years of living with them, Cindy approached me and gave me a year's notice to move. Their little girls were no longer little, and they needed my room.

Moving to Colorado was one of the highlights of my life. No more crowded freeways, high crime rate, big-city noise and smog, and confusion. I looked for work in Eagle and found one at the local airport where I've worked now for four different companies in the past eight years. The commercial part of the airport is open only during ski season for four months when we bring in a thousand people a day to ski. In April, we're furloughed until the following November when the ski season opens up again for the winter months. After being furloughed, we all went back to our summer jobs: golf course maintenance, firefighting, or working as fishing guides, or at a local ranch.

Colorado is hunting country, and all of the locals know exactly where to go to bag their elk. I have no trouble filling my freezer with elk during hunting season, whether I hunt or not. My friends who are hunters are very generous. And besides, my doctor tells me that elk's meat is the healthiest because of its low cholesterol.

I've videoed cowboys as they branded their livestock in the spring. It takes about three or four grown men to hold down a calf while the iron, heated red hot, is applied to the rump of the calf. All of the full-grown cows, hundreds of them, are penned together, mooing for their babies. Once the baby has been branded, it's released back to its mother who will find it among hundreds of cows.

I'm getting used to people in the supermarket or the post office or on the street smiling and saying "howdy" to me. A total stranger.

Once the sun goes down and the sidewalks are rolled up, the residents here in Eagle go to bed early, all except for the Brush Creek Saloon where real cowboy's hangout. They're a joyful bunch.

There are two well-needed stoplights in Eagle, a supermarket, a pharmacy, a library, a senior center, and a brand-new movie theater. The movie theater is in a part of town that used to be a cattle ranch with thousands of head of cattle. Developers discovered it and saw the potential for erecting homes. They had plans for over twelve hundred homes to be built. With all of the homes being constructed, I still favor my little plot of land here in Eagle.

I didn't move to Colorado to be close to relatives. It just happened that way. First, I located Cousin Willie and his daughter, Michelle. I made several trips to Denver to see Willie. His health was deteriorating, and I wanted to have lunch with him and Cousin Delores. Delores had several children that I got to know, and there was Cousin Ken and his wife Bonnie and Ken's mother who lived in Kimball, Nebraska. When Willie passed away, cousins came from Omaha and Missouri and other towns from Midwestern United States.

I hadn't seen cousins Don and Allan Nimmer for many years, but we became reacquainted at Willie's funeral and have kept in touch. They are my second cousins. Originally, there were four brothers and a sister: Wolf, Joseph, George, Eli, and Anna. Wolf had eleven children. All but three have passed away. Joseph had six children. All have passed away. George didn't have any children. Eli had two boys. One had passed away. I am the only surviving child, and Anna had nine children, of which only four have survived at this time. George Nimmer, Don, and Allan's brother couldn't make it to the funeral. I contacted him recently after not seeing him for about forty-five years and said on the phone, "Betcha don't know who this is?" His immediate reply was "Howard?" After forty years, I couldn't believe it.

I'm in touch with cousins both from my mother's and father's sides. We've all become Americanized. Cousins Willie and Mike both fought bravely in World War II for the Allies. They both left children who survived them. All of Uncle Joe's family had passed on. Uncle Joe's oldest son, George, had a machine shop in Omaha during the war and supplied materials to the American war effort. After George had passed away, his son, Ken, took over the reigns and became president of George Risk Industries in Kimball, Nebraska. Uncle Wolf's family moved to California and became involved in show business. My brother became a pilot for Flying Tigers and raised eight children. I've become quite close to Aunt Anna's surviving children, at least on the phone. They're wonderfully warm people.

Cousin Terry called to tell me that my brother's oldest daughter, Kari, was married and would like to see me. It had been forty years. I called, and we both cried. They came to Eagle to see me. She wanted to know what happened to our relationship. I explained what her mother had done to me. She was not the least bit surprised.

APPENDIX A

One person that I intentionally left out of this writing is my brother, Russell. Whenever my mother visited him and his wife, she left feeling sad and angry. I'm sure my brother treated mother with love and consideration. My sister-in-law treated her in just the opposite manner. I was outside my brother's house working on my car when my brother invited me to come in and have dinner with them. No sooner had we sat down than she stood up and began screaming and yelling obscenities at me. She called me every SOB name she could think of. That was just the beginning. She got louder and used unbelievable curse words. I looked to my brother for help. He had lowered his head and continued eating his spaghetti. I realized then that he was afraid of her. I got up and passed her running to the door while she was still screaming. As I drove home, I wondered what I had done. Maybe she had a bad day, and there would surely be an apology. Weeks and months and years have passed. I've never heard a single word from them in forty years. She has no class.

My brother grew up and went roller-skating with a real clean crowd from school. At a young age, I hung out in nightclubs and with motorcycle riders. When I was to appear in federal court, I got off the elevator in the federal building and was surprised to see Russ sitting on the stairs waiting to go into the courthouse. There was some sort of a bond. Like my mother's family, we didn't have much to say to each other, and we showed no love to each other. We just accepted each other. I had no desire to get close to anyone. I often wonder what life would have been like if my dad had lived and my mother had stayed home.

APPENDIX B

Through a growing process of many years, my Bible has become my most prized possession. I studied it and found no contradiction. The Bible truly is the Word of God. I don't deserve heaven, but God in his mercy has granted me a place there. I used to go out with people in my church and visit people who had visited our church. There were two questions that we would ask them. The first was "Have you reached a place in your spiritual life where you know for certain that if you died tonight, you would go to heaven?" You'd be surprised at the answers that we got. Question number two was "If you were to stand before God and he asked you, 'Why should I let you into my heaven?' what would you say?" Dynamite questions. We would back up the answers with the Bible!

APPENDIX C

I've tried to keep my autobiography as factual as possible, but over time—just as in criminal cases—some facts have become slightly blurred, especially after forty-five or fifty-five years. Some major events had to be omitted because of the harm it might cause to some people. Other bad events had to be omitted because of possible retaliation against me. I don't want to be looking over my shoulder for the rest of my life.

BVG